Human Design
& Health

Other titles by Eleanor Haspel-Portner

The Triple Design Matrix
Beyond Human Design
Cosmic Guidance for Mastering Your Life
Cosmic Secrets
Astrology Essentials
First Degree Reiki Manual
Second Degree Reiki Manual & Workbook
Marriage in Trouble: A Time of Decision

Human Design & Health

A PRACTITIONER'S GUIDE TO THE BASICS

Ra Uru Hu
Eleanor Haspel-Portner, PhD
Marvin Portner, MD

Human Design and Health
by Eleanor Haspel-Portner

Copyright © 2025 Noble Sciences, LLC.

All rights reserved.
No part of this publication may be reproduced, transmitted, transcribed, stored in a retrieval system, or translated into any other language or computer language in whole or in part, in any form or by any means, whether electronic, mechanical, magnetic, optical, manual, or otherwise, without the prior consent of the publisher except for the use of brief quotations in a book review.

Library of Congress Control Number: 2025906206

ISBNs:
978-1-931053-22-8 (Paperback)
978-1-931053-21-1 (Ebook)

BODY, MIND & SPIRIT / Human Design
PSYCHOLOGY / Personality
HEALTH & FITNESS / Alternative Therapies
BODY, MIND & SPIRIT / New Thought
SELF-HELP / Personal Growth / Success

Book Design by Michelle M. White

Author's websites
www.nobleenergywellness.com
www.DrEleanor.com
www.moptu.com/DrEleanor

Published by Noble Sciences, LLC
Mount Pleasant SC

> Our primary goal at Rave Life Sciences is to make Human Design & Health information available as quickly as possible to the public and professionals. This module is not a perfectly constructed text; it is a preliminary text for practical use.
>
> Publisher's note: This book is not intended to replace a one-on-one relationship with a qualified healthcare professional and is not intended as medical advice. It is a sharing of knowledge and information from the research and experience of the authors. You are advised and encouraged to consult with your health care professional with regard to matters relating to your health, and in particular regarding symptoms that may require diagnosis or immediate attention.

*To Ra Uru Hu (Alan "Robert" Krakower),
who entrusted me with documenting the science
of Human Design and introducing the Dream Rave.
I am ever grateful for this multidimensional data
that validates the Four Worlds of Consciousness
and Noble Energy Maps®, which have
the potential to change how we understand
consciousness and communication.*

*To my dear husband and soulmate,
Marvin M. Portner, M.D.,
you inspire and encourage me to always
be my best self. Your recognition and understanding
of our creative process and the importance of our work
have allowed us both to flourish. I am deeply humbled
and blessed to always have you by my side.*

Table of Contents

Preface to this Edition by Dr. Eleanor®   xi

Preface to the Original Monographs
on Human Design and Health   xv

Statement of Purpose   xix

Foreword   xxi

Introduction to Human Design
1

The Four [Five] Types
7

The Nine Centers
33

Overview of Profiles
99

Looking at Lines
105

Closing
127

About the Author   131

Go Beyond Human Design with
Dr. Eleanor's® Noble Energy Map®   133

Table of Figures

Figure 1: The Mandala of Synthesis® 4

Figure 2: Personality and Design Calculations 5

Figure 3: The Manifestor 10

Figure 4: The Generator 15

Figure 5: The Projector 21

Figure 6: The Reflector 29

Figure 7: The Centers Labeled 34

Figure 8: The 9 Centers 35

Figure 9: The Head Center 37

Figure 10: The Ajna Center 42

Figure 11: The Throat Center 44

Figure 12: The G or Self Center 48

Figure 13: The Heart Center 52

Figure 14: The Sacral Center 59

Figure 15: The Splenic Center 69

Figure 16: The Solar Plexus 77

Figure 17: The Root Center 92

Figure 18: Format Energies 93

Figure 19: The Line Geometry Graph (Profile) 101

Preface
to this Edition by Dr. Eleanor®

It is my great honor and privilege to share my knowledge with you and to use it to help you live a life of fulfillment and recognition of your divinity.

My interest in astrology began in 1971 when I was told that astrology is the most scientific of the esoteric disciplines. At the time, I had just completed my doctorate at the University of Chicago, was well versed in psychology, sociology, anthropology, and biology, and had done extensive research on world religions; however, hearing that astrology was scientific intrigued me.

I found an astrology bookstore near my home and proceeded to learn how to calculate an astrology chart. It proved to be the hardest thing I had ever attempted to learn. The language was symbolic and the mathematical calculations complex. But I persisted and began to understand basic astrological work.

Two years later, I was deeply honored and blessed to book an astrological reading with Katherine de Jersey. The reading with her showed me the power and depth of astrology in the hands of a Master. I studied astrology privately with several astrologers and was also in training as a Jungian Analyst. I also focused on Kundalini energy and meditation because I was having Kundalini energy experiences, and I wanted to understand them and my psychic abilities.

In 1996, I encountered the Human Design Mandala, a complex, yet intriguing system that intertwines psychology, astrology, and developmental science. My fascination with the Human Design System deepened with each passing year.

Through my research, I had a staggering revelation: 99% of humanity possesses the inherent potential to manifest their true selves. Tragically, the majority of people remain oblivious to the existence of the Four Worlds — the Mental, Spiritual, Emotional, and Physical dimensions that govern our daily reality.

While their lack of awareness is not inherently "bad," it is a missed opportunity for growth and fulfillment. When individuals are unaware of the Four Worlds, they navigate life without understanding the diverse dimensions of their consciousness. They may feel disconnected, struggling to align actions with their true selves, and miss out on the profound impact that recognizing and harmonizing with these dimensions can have on their overall wellbeing.

It was then that my mission crystallized in my mind: to illuminate these dimensions, to guide individuals towards a conscious existence that embraces the essence of their soul.

Preface

to the Original Monographs on Human Design and Health

In 1999, Ra Uru Hu asked Marvin and me to document the Human Design System and to do so separately from the Human Design Community. Ra's intention was for Marvin and me to form a professional community, where we would apply our clinical and statistical research expertise to the Human Design System so it would be validated.

At the time I began studying Human Design in 1996, Ra stated clearly that the primary information he was given by "the Voice" was primarily the body graph and its measurements. Over the next several years, I was present when Ra interpreted the body graphs. Much of what Ra taught has proved to be useful, but much has not held true to the scrutiny of science.

Based on Ra's request, Marvin and I took on the task of validating Human Design scientifically. As a social scientist, psychologist, astrologer, and trained in the Tree of Life, I embarked on the research project that has been my focus for over twenty years. Often, it is only in retrospect that we fully understand our process. Ra wanted my work to be separate from Human Design because consciousness in 2000 was not yet ready to embrace a far more extensive system that goes Beyond Human Design. By continuing clinical research without input from the Human Design community, I documented additional calculations that include the way humans process multidimensional information and detailed developmental critical times in early human development.

For the past twenty years, I have studied many aspects of the body's energy maps, recognizing how they interact and synthesize information across the Four Worlds. As a practicing clinician, I have performed Noble Energy Maps® on all of my clients, both past and present. I compared their characteristics and information-processing methods to assess the validity and reliability of Noble Energy Maps®. Over the years, I have analyzed 15,000 maps and am continually amazed by their accuracy. Early in my professional career, I taught psychological testing at the college level. Noble Energy Maps® provide a more revealing and accurate personality profile than any psychological test I have encountered in the field of psychology.

In October 2022, during an important time in my life, I recognized correlations between the formatted layout of Noble Energy Maps® and the Infinity Sign or Figure 8. This recognition integrated my work with the Four Worlds taught in many disciplines, especially in the Kabbalistic Tree of Life. Once the integration of the Four Worlds as a way of transforming consciousness and helping individuals live and manifest their full potential became clear to me, I knew it was time to re-release the books I wrote with Ra Uru Hu along with the results of my statistical and clinical research.

The original transcripts form the basis of this book. I also added personal information about my relationship with Ra, commentaries, and clinical observations on the research, indicated by the blue text. When Ra and I presented the information about Human Design, it was clear that it was a hypothetical and not a proven system. When the Voice gave Ra the body graph over five days, it did not give him any interpretations. The Body Graph had to be exact, and Ra told me that he struggled over the five days to draw it exactly the way the Voice wanted it to be. The original Body Graph is drawn to scale and reflects its sacred geometry as in the Tree of Life. During my partnership with Ra, our legal agreement gave me the copyrights to the

Body Graph and all materials and information given to Marvin and me by Ra. When Ra began to teach from the Body Graph, he formed hypotheses that he taught as fact.

Ra knew that much of what he was teaching would not hold up scientifically, and it is to his credit that, ultimately, he wanted the system he was gifted to be valid, reliable, and proven. Ra had the foresight to put Marvin and me in charge of the scientific validation of the system and introduced the general public to a simple formulaic way of understanding the basics of the Human Design System.

In 2022, I was guided to release nearly thirty years of research on Human Design and Noble Energy Maps® that go beyond Human Design.

Since this book is source material, I did not edit any original language when updating it. Maintaining the integrity of source material is a substantial value of mine, and in that vein, I kept Ra's work intact. Based on clinical and statistical observations, I have noted where I evolved my thinking. While editing and reviewing this material, I felt great gratitude and respect for the work Ra and I jointly did. I am especially indebted to Ra for bringing my awareness of the Four Worlds to consciousness and providing a system I could use to verify and document how the Four Worlds function.

The black text in this book is a synthesis of the original three books in the *Monographs on Human Design and Health* series published by Rave Life Sciences. It combines the content of *Module 1: Types, Centers Profiles and Lines, Introductory Primer 1: Types, and Introductory Primer 2: Centers* into one comprehensive tool. My current commentary is indicated by the text in blue.

May you be empowered by your inner spirit and live your dreams.
Dr. Eleanor®
Mount Pleasant, SC
2025

Statement of Purpose

With the Human and Mammalian Design Information as well as other ancillary knowledge given to him in his trust, Ra Uru Hu carries the responsibility to ensure that this knowledge is disseminated and validated with integrity and professionalism. This knowledge is a true synthesis of science and spirit and, as such, needs verification. It is not a belief system but a testable logic system that is being proved. Ra Uru Hu oversees the integrity of design as transmitted to him in 1987. He brings forth the information as it is appropriate and teaches the application of it in its form and structure. The dissemination of this information in its true form is the essence of the purpose of his work.

Rave Life Sciences is dedicated to the dissemination of information to healthcare professionals and to those whose professional responsibilities concern the health and well-being of their "Patients" and "Clients." The focus and purpose of Rave Life Sciences is the integration of Design and its information with day-to-day client concerns, leading to an ever deeper and broader recognition of its personal and professional value.

The experiential aspect of living with the information is under the guidance of Marvin M. Portner, M.D. He integrates Design into his holistic medical practice by using the Body Graphs of his patients to help determine areas of vulnerability and appropriate treatments. He is involved in validating and documenting case material and embryological development in accordance with Design information. Marvin M. Portner, M.D. is available for clinical consultations, integrating this information with his solid base in medicine.

How living one's design affects health and psyche is clinically documented and impacted through experiences, understanding, and knowledge. Rave Life Sciences' task is to make this information available to professionals for their use and the use of their patient/client base. Eleanor Haspel-Portner, Ph.D., teaches the application of design in people's lives. She does individual readings and works with couples, groups, and parents. She is working with families and businesses in the application and documentation of the value of design in successful healthy living. She is responsible for the social scientific studies that will be published shortly. Because of the necessity, at this point, to document all the work with scientifically valid studies and research, we are working with many groups to educate them on the possibilities open to them and allow participation in pilot studies by those who are interested in working with us. Eleanor Haspel-Portner, PhD. is designing and developing these programs. She is available to help design programs that utilize design applications and to consult with individuals regarding their life paths.

In addition, Rave Life Sciences is working to create a foundation of design-aware professionals by documenting research and application of design in various settings. Only through the verification of applications and their validity can we state clearly and scientifically that this is a logical, testable system that proves capable of supporting and enhancing health, consciousness, and the well-being of humans and mammals, in fact, of all life forms. As part of this research and application program, training programs are being developed by Ra Uru Hu, Marvin M. Portner, M.D., and Eleanor Haspel-Portner, Ph.D., so the work can be carried into the marketplace and all areas of life and health.

Rave Life Sciences educates professionals interested in incorporating design into their own lives and in the care and health of their clients or patients. As part of this effort, Rave Life Sciences is developing a publishing program that will offer modules to share didactic information about the design process in health and related fields. As the information is documented and validated, both research and teaching modules will be made available.

Areas being developed include Rave Biology, including Rave Medicine, Rave Anatomy, Physiology, and Embryology; Rave Psychology, including DreamRave Analysis and Design, Family Analysis, Organizational Analysis, Business Applications, Communication Applications, Mammalian Design and its applications for Veterinarians and Breeders. How design can and will be applied to facilitating the communication of consciousness and health at the foundational level of human and mammalian life is the basic purpose of Rave Life Sciences. Research monographs outlining studies and the statistical methodology and findings will also be published. The data is currently being gathered and is under analysis.

> Although the Human Design Community was not fully open to embracing Rave Life Sciences' findings, I continued to document the science clinically, using the body map in the Four Worlds. This work stands up to clinical scrutiny. It has empowered many individuals who intuitively knew that the Human Design System is a partial system. The Human Design System taught by Ra did not integrate the Kabbalistic Tree of Life, astrology, and developmental critical times in a person's life. I am a social scientist versed in all these systems. Thus, Noble Energy Maps® provides an expansion and integrates all dimensions and systems into its work.

Audio/visual learning tools will be available as part of the training program and disseminating this material to interested individuals and groups. Tapes from seminars, as well as videos, will be sold.

Ra Uru Hu
Marvin Portner, M.D.
Eleanor Haspel-Portner, Ph.D.

Foreword

While we at Rave Life Sciences are primarily focused on the education of professionals who affect the lives and the health of their patients and clients, we are acutely aware of this information's practical value and application. Until now, the information has been available to those who had private readings or consultations and those who wanted to study Human Design in more depth. With the founding of Rave Life Sciences, a whole new chapter in disseminating this information and knowledge has begun. Enough documentation of the basis of this information and knowledge exists to make it essential for the information to reach as many people as quickly as possible for the benefit of everyone. Rave Life Sciences is putting together modules (monographs) for professionals. At the same time, Rave Life Sciences is releasing companion information for practical use and application in the lives of the people with whom those professionals work.

This information is simple, straightforward, and understandable to everyone. It is based on your Design and is something you can take in, try, and live with. You are already living in your body with your energy mechanics. Now you can have a tool that can tell you how that body is designed and how it is meant to run. Design is the map. Once you have the map and spend a little time learning the terminology, you can begin to know, understand, and experience how it works. You learn to know and be who you are. The journey into the knowledge of oneself is ancient. However, that journey now happens with some simple tools that can change your life, your health, and your family's health forever. It occurs without therapy, drugs, or pain. It happens by knowing how you are designed and by living who you really are. Enjoy the journey and love yourself.

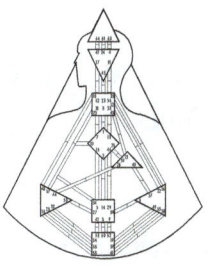

Introduction to Human Design

This primer will take you through the basic language you need to understand your own Design Body Graph and will demonstrate to you some of the health applications that can benefit you and your loved ones immediately. By having the map of who you are and the map of those you relate to daily, you truly live your nature and enjoy a level of health and psychological well-being that is your destiny. The journey begins here. As in all journeys, the first time you are exposed to the terrain can feel unfamiliar. But after you gain some familiarity, it is an easy trip. Design is like that. It is inherently simple and very understandable. But this is your first trip. Be patient with yourself until you finish this primer. The patience will be worthwhile and your life will be immeasurably enriched.

What is a Human Design Chart

Conception begins the ongoing process that culminates in birth. At birth, with the infant separated from the mother, an imprint occurs, which manifests as the personality of an individual. This personality is not the whole of the person. A person is much more than the sum of their parts. [We now know that a baby continues developing exponentially during their first three months of life.

During this time, there are critical developmental markers that anchor the energy of the Four Worlds into the baby's aura or energetic field. At three months, babies are capable of choosing what they relate to and what they avoid.]

A Human Design Rave [Mental World] chart shows the flow of energy in a person both consciously and unconsciously. This energy flow is consistent for that individual, is based on their genetics, and exists for their lifetime. When an individual knows, understands, and experiences who they are with clarity and as separate from the environmental and personal influences, they appreciate the integrity of their very nature. When individuals live with whom they are not, they experience all kinds of discomforts, psychological disharmony, physical illness, and experiences that are not right for them in their lives. [These statements are true, but remember, Ra was only using the Mental/Waking World Type.]

Prevention is the key. By knowing who you are through knowing your Design, you can live your full potential. Design is for everyone. This knowledge is not a belief system but rather a provable logical system based on your genetic code. [Currently, the Human Design field that teaches only the Mental/Waking World Chart is an incomplete system and, thus, can be misleading.] As you work with the knowledge of your Design, you experience its truth. You feel the rightness of living who you are. You become increasingly able to know and communicate in your own unique way. You become aware of situations when you are with individuals who do not honor your nature. This system allows individual differences with no judgment because we are all designed to be ourselves and to honor the selves of others. [Please honor your feelings if you are told something that does not align with what you know and sense about yourself.]

Esoteric literature always emphasizes that we must know ourselves first and that we are the microcosm for the macrocosm. Design is the living knowledge, experience, and feeling of that fact. It makes esoteric knowledge real. It is not a belief system. The experience of living with the map of who you really are results in awareness and consciousness that opens you to the full potential of yourself and the others around you.

Human Design is a treasure map that is available now to anyone who wants to see it and who is interested in learning how to read it and its terrain. This map is a map of yourself. [The Human Design map is one-eighth of the information needed to describe how you function based on cosmic energy and how you are designed to manifest your true potential.] It is real and concrete, yet it is what all the esoteric disciplines talked about being elusive. It was elusive because the map was not readily available. Each individual has a different map that can easily be calculated and shown to them. Once you have your map, you need to learn how to read it. It is no more difficult than it was to learn to read when you were a child. The purpose of this primer is to give you a beginning lesson in reading the map so you can begin to know yourself as you truly are.

By knowing how you are energetically designed, you also know the experience of how you change when you are in the presence of others who have their own unique Design. Forces over which we have no control condition us all. We move within a universe, and to the degree that we move in harmony with our own Design in that universe, we are at one with it. To the degree that we do not live who we are designed to be, we live in disharmony and suffer the consequences.

Design Basics

The Human Design Mandala of Synthesis® (Figure 1) shows the individual body graph with its nine centers, 64 Gates, and 36 Channels connecting them. The Circle around the body graph is the 360-degree Zodiac circle. The Zodiac degrees correspond to the lines of the specific hexagrams of the I-Ching. Every 5 degrees 37 minutes and 30 seconds of arc, another hexagram is activated in the zodiac.

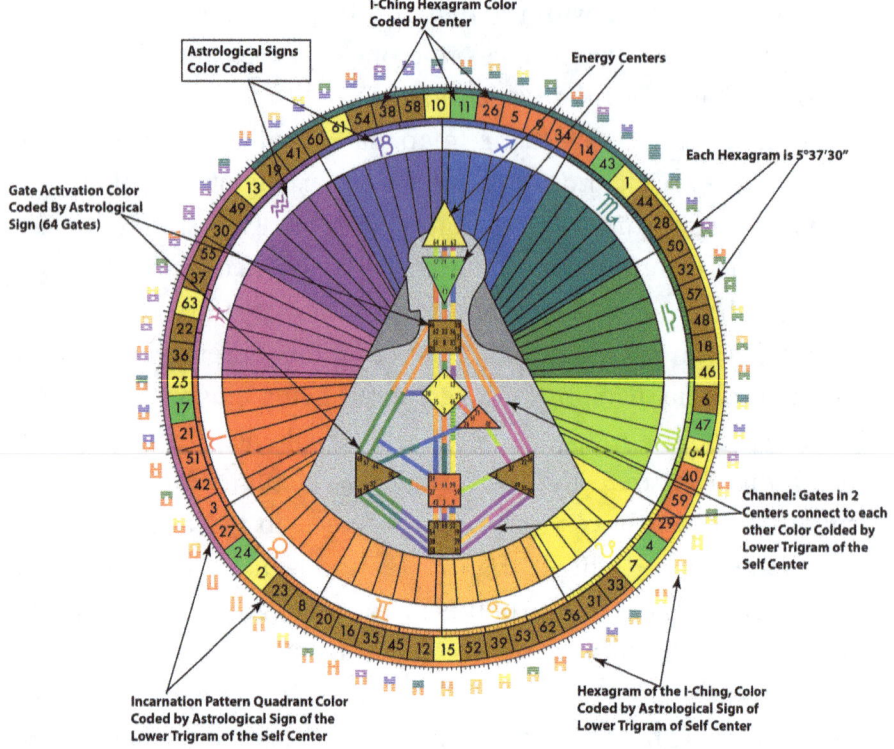

Figure 1: The Mandala of Synthesis®

The math of the 64 gates of the I-Ching hexagrams is congruent with the genetic code of the human being. Thus, by translating the zodiac degrees to the hexagrams of the I-Ching and its lines and then coloring in those gates and channels in the body graph, we have an energy map of an individual. This energy map is astoundingly accurate. [The Human Design Mental/Waking World Chart is only a partial picture of who you are.]

Two calculations are made that determine what gates are active in an individual's body graph (Figure 2). The first calculation is based on the time and place of that person's birth. This calculation gives us the gates of the Personality Design of that person. The gates corresponding to the zodiac degrees for this time are transposed into the body graph in black and show the conscious personality of the Design. A second calculation is made that shows the design when the unconscious is laid down in the fetus; this calculation is for a chart 88 solar degrees (about 3 months or 88 days) before birth.

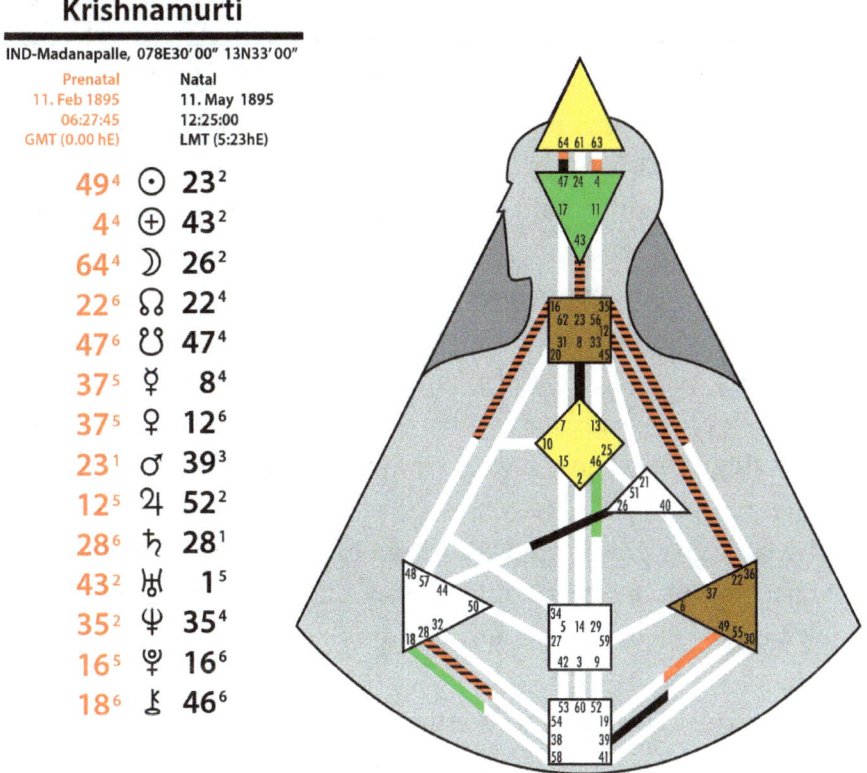

Figure 2: Personality and Design Calculations

This specific time shows the unconscious or what we call the Design [Prenatal] calculation. The gates corresponding to the zodiac positions at this time are put into the body graph in red and tell us how that person functions on the unconscious level of their being. [It is more accurate to describe the prenatal calculation as showing when the cortex of the fetus at the beginning of the third trimester of pregnancy began to register information that it would respond to after birth. Brain scans confirm this time as critical in human development.]

We thus, have a body graph with black and red coloring. Two gates that connect on either end, we call definition or a defined channel. This definition results in a whole channel being activated. This activation, or definition, is a connection within an individual that is always turned on and can always be relied on in that individual. These channels that are defined or not make us feel as we feel. A lot of what we experience when we talk about how we feel or what we know ourselves to be is describing our definitions and activations in our energy system. When a channel is defined, the two centers on either end of the channel are colored in to show that the center is active.

The centers are energy vortexes in the body. They are similar to the chakras in the Hindu system but are not exactly the same. The energy centers, nine of them, each have different functions, which determine a great deal about the way in which the individual uses their energy in the world and with others. The body graph, or energy map of the body, shows where connections are made and where the power sources of energy exist for an individual. The body graph describes or gives us a diagram of our vehicle and how it is designed. It is actually like an instruction book that, once understood, can be utilized by us for the proper functioning of our vehicle on all levels. Design is actually mechanical, not interpretive. [Because the defined channels are based on our interpretation of the I-Ching, its astrological, and Kabbalistic interpretations, your design is interpretive.] Once we know that about ourselves, we can live that nature and value it for what it provides. We can also know where we are open to being conditioned or influenced by the energies of others, as well as how we condition and influence others. [Centers that remain open or are not activated by a planet show that you experience all the energies and can respond to them with all possibilities open to you. At times, open centers make you vulnerable to picking up energy from those people around you.]

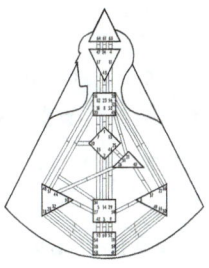

The Four [Five] Types

Most crucial to the application of Human Design principles in your life and living truly who you are is an understanding of Type. Specifically, you need to understand your own Type. If all you gain from your contact with Human Design and its application to your health is an understanding of your type and how to live your Type, it will change your life. If you understand and know your Type and go to the next step, which is to understand and know the Types of members of your family, you will experience a new level of respect and appreciation for who you are living with and how you and they impact each other.

In Design, the map for each individual is unique. For you, in your knowledge, understanding, and experience of Design right now, it is most important to know your Type. Four Types [we now know there are five] are possible in Design: [the Manifesting Generator], the Manifestor, the Generator, the Projector, and the Reflector. These [five rather than] four Types represent the way you face and meet the world. The [Manifesting Generator], Manifestor, and the Generator are considered energy Types, while the Projector and the Reflector are considered non-energy Types.

Type is derived directly from the definition in the Rave chart [Human Design Mental/Waking World Chart.] Type is important because it tells a lot about the theme underlying the nature of an individual. Both the Throat Center and Sacral Center play key roles. To be an energy Type, one must have a defined Sacral Center and/or have a Motor (fuel) Center connected to the Throat Center, either directly or indirectly. There are four motors in the body: The Sacral Center, the primary life force energy; the Heart Center, the ego and power [Calling the Heart Center an Ego Center is misleading from a psychological perspective], the Root Center, the adrenal pressure; and the Solar Plexus Center, the emotional system.

Type is very important in health. Different diseases affect each Type differently; each Type heals or benefits differently from healing remedies, medicines, or other treatments. When you know your Design and your true nature, you know how to live a healthy life for yourself. No one else is designed exactly as you are, both in terms of your biology and in terms of your conditioning. Thus, knowing your Design and observing yourself is key to your own integrity as a healthy person. It is essential to learn to enter into things correctly according to your Type. [Because Type operates over time as a baby develops, it is essential to know what turns on and what turns off as we look at the charts over the 6-month period between three months before and three months after birth. Your Human Design Type is limited to the Mental/Waking World and does not show how you make choices or function as an integrated complex person.]

Everything about design in terms of medicine and health is about prevention; it is all too late when it is about curing. Again, it goes back to the nature of the person. Know your design — know how to deal with your health. Know your patient's design — know how to deal with their health.

The real work is to get patients to recognize the basics of their own Type. Recognition of Type is very simple. If patients can experiment with that, they can see that it is part of their healing process. When someone comes to you who is already ill, getting that person to see their Type is part of the cure, along with whatever you give them to deal with what has happened to them. You can start them on the path of being healthy by telling them about their Type. [This statement about Type is misleading. In my research on Type over the past 25 years, I found that ninety-nine percent of the population in their Noble Energy Maps® are Manifesting Generators. Thus, to tell someone that they are a certain Type based only on their Mental/Waking Design is misleading and can be disempowering if that is all the information given to them.]

Rave Life Sciences educates and trains health facilitators because that is the real work of healing. Its goal is to help people in the health field understand themselves and apply their valuable knowledge individually rather than generalizing it.

When a patient comes to your door, whether [Manifesting Generator], Manifestor, Generator, Projector, or Reflector, depending on the nature of their illness, a proper healing direction can be established according to their Type. Their individual nature, how the disease came into their life, and why it was there in the first place are aspects that can be seen just from looking at their chart. This is an invisible factor for most people.

[My research completed in 1999 definitively documented five Types.] Two are energy Types, and two are non-energy Types. The Manifestor and the Generator are energy Types. [The Manifesting Generator was shown to be a Type independent of the other four Types. Thus, there are three energy Types and two non-energy Types.]

> According to the statistics, 8% of the population are Manifestors, 36.8% are Generators, 20.9% are Projectors, 0.9% are Reflectors, and 33.5% are Manifesting Generators. It is now documented that 99% of the Population are Manifesting Generators at three months of age in their Integrated Noble Energy Maps®.
>
> (Preliminary Research on the Human Design System and Health. Eleanor Haspel-Portner, Ph.D., Ra Uru Hu, Marvin Portner, M.D., Erik Memmert, Charles Haspel. 2000-2003).

The Energy Types: The Manifestor and The Generator

The Manifestor

The Manifestor (see Figure 3) is a person who has their Throat Center connected to a motor either directly or indirectly. There are four motors in the body: The Sacral Center — the primary life force - and the Heart Center — ego and willpower [using the terms ego and willpower are misleading and incorrect in this context. Ego is a psychological term that refers to the way we function in the Mental/Waking World when we navigate our day-to-day life. The Heart Center has power because it is the heart muscle itself, and it brings our life force energy to us from the Divine. It is, thus, a strong power center that motivates us toward creative intelligence.], the Root Center — adrenal pressure, and the Solar Plexus Center — emotions.

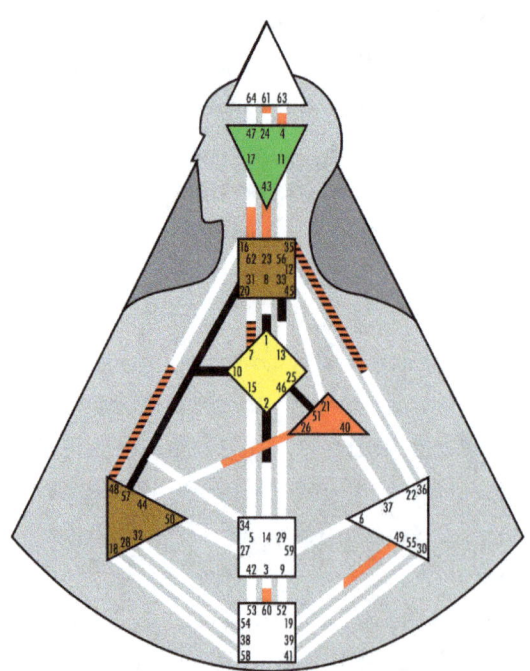

Figure 3: The Manifestor

THE FOUR [FIVE] TYPES

Because the Manifestor is an energy Type, the Manifestor can always manifest. The throat is the center of manifestation in the human being. When the throat is connected to a motor, that person is always able to act "to do." Depending on which centers are connected to the Throat Center and by what route makes people different and gives flavor to the manifestation. However, the basic idea for you to grasp at this point is that some people are Designed to be Manifestors, and others are not.

Because Manifestors generally encounter so much resistance in their lives, they tend to be angry Types. [There is no evidence of a Manifestor or Manifesting Generator being an "angry" Type.] In order to eliminate resistance, the Manifestor has to ask permission and inform others before acting. For a Manifestor to be healthy, it is critical for them to learn how to eliminate resistance from their lives. [Some Manifestors and Manifesting Generators may be pushy. However, since most of the population are Manifesting Generators in their integrated consciousness, the key is learning how you integrate energy patterns from each world and how to communicate effectively for yourself. The statistical data does not support the personality characteristics attributed by Ra to the different Types.]

Think about the way in which we condition our children to always "do." Think about how badly you often feel if you "do not do enough." Not everyone is designed "to do." [Most people are designed as Manifesting Generators.] In fact, Manifestors are not a majority in the population; they are relatively uncommon as a Type. [99% of the population are Manifesting Generators in their Integrated Design] Nevertheless, we, as human beings, identify manifestation as an archetype of a successful person. In our society, someone who accomplishes a lot of things is considered successful. If you are not a Manifestor, trying to be one will make you sick. [We have no data on this statement.]

Once you know if you are or are not a Manifestor, it may be much easier for you to understand what you are easily able or not able "to do." Moreover, if you have a child who is a Manifestor, teach that child to inform you of what that child wants "to do" because it is natural for the child to just be active without asking or telling anyone what is going on. Manifestor children are especially sensitive to being treated with disrespect or rudeness; they do not ever forget the experience. They get punished repeatedly for simply being themselves, active individuals who get things done. When a Manifestor child is told to wait or "not to do," or is punished because they did the "wrong" thing, they become angry; that is their nature, it is not their "fault," it is just the way they are. People need to be treated with respect for their type to be true to their real nature. Accordingly, if your child is not a Manifestor, do not expect action independently of interaction. [We have no evidence to support this interpretation of a Manifestor child.]

Often, at school or in seminars, people are told that they "should" be able to go out and take action. This is not a true statement and does great harm to the self-esteem of many people. If you are a Manifestor, you can always act; in fact, if you are a Manifestor, you may have great difficulty asking for help even when you need it. You need to look at that in yourself. Learn to inform others of what you are doing. Let them know what you are doing so you eliminate the resistance you have become so accustomed to meeting in your life.

Think about what it means to be a Manifestor in terms of your health. As a Manifestor, because you are not used to asking for help, illness may explode upon you. You do not ask for help immediately because you generally assume that you can deal with things yourself. As you become educated about the centers of your body, you will understand how your type affects your health and how disease may come into your body. You will begin to learn ways to avoid such vulnerability. If you have a child who is a Manifestor, understand that this child will not easily ask for help from you or anyone else. This child will want to do things on its own. Offer help and recognize the delicacy of the need for Manifestors to be asked what they are feeling and what they want. [Manifestors inform

THE FOUR [FIVE] TYPES

others of their feelings and their actions, and they do not ask for help in the way we generally expect it to be done.]

> As a Manifestor in my basic Human Design Mental/Waking World Chart, I often told Ra that I did not fit his description of a Manifestor. In fact, I did not initiate action quickly and always asked for help when I needed it. In fact, I am a strong Lunar Generator who becomes a Manifesting Generator in my Integrated Design. Understanding yourself is far more important than any description imposed upon you. Listen to your inner self rather than what someone tells you about yourself.

Manifestors are subject to heart attacks. If you see a Manifestor who has an undefined Heart Center, then you know that you are with a person who is a "walking potential heart attack." You know that the heart can just explode, and you know that when this Manifestor gets that first pain, they are not calling out for help. They are not saying, "There is something wrong with me." If they did call out for help, the chances are that they could be helped, but they rarely do. [In research on 5,000 heart attack patients, there were no statistical differences in people who died of a heart attack who had an open Heart Center compared to a defined Heart Center. Thus, this statement by Ra is unsubstantiated and is, in fact, false.]

In Manifestors, the disease seems to jump out. These are the people who appear to get spontaneously ill. They walk along like everything is fine, and all of a sudden, "bang," it hits them. They always try to push the problem aside because resistance is natural for the Manifestor. A patient who is a Manifestor has their immune system under attack because they are always meeting resistance. That is why Manifestors are not common in the population. They are useful, but they are not common. [Manifestors are defined based on astrological forces and not on their behavior or their characteristics. Attributing illness or personality characteristics to them denies the possibility that each Manifestor has choices, and consciousness overrides definition.]

The immune system of the Manifestor always has to be of primary concern because they always face resistance. If you have a Manifestor with a defined Splenic Center, they are designed to be able to deal with the resistance. They have a natural way to deal with it, but it also means that their immune system is the kind that can collapse spontaneously. They are overtired, overworked, and over-processing. Manifestors are vulnerable in that sense. They go, go, go until they drop. [Not all Manifestors "go until they drop". As a Manifestor in my Human Design Mental/Waking World Chart, I do not fit this description. I have a clear sense of my limits and do not overwork or overprocess. It is the Lunar Generator aspect of my Four Worlds Charts that protects me from overwork and overdoing. Thus, recognizing that inner knowing is more powerful than any one chart is critical to communicate to clients.]

When you see a Manifestor with an undefined Splenic Center, you see someone who can get very ill and not have the natural equipment to deal with it. [Anyone with an open Splenic Center picks up energy on a physical level from people around them. For the Manifestor, this empathic sensitivity may push them toward being a caretaker, or if they are unaware of their capacity to pick up energy from the people around them, they may feel overloaded and overwhelmed. Conscious awareness of their vulnerabilities helps transform these vulnerabilities and diminishes the overload. Manifestors with a defined Solar Plexus Center and an undefined Splenic Center need to be educated on the mechanics of the emotional wave; otherwise, they often encounter real trouble. All people who have a defined Solar Plexus Center do well when they recognize that Emotional Reactivity can only be transformed through the Spiritual/Archetypal World and through the transformation of reactivity into a higher frequency vibration.] These are people who have anger sickness. Their anger makes them ill. [We have no evidence that these statements are valid.]

All centers in the body have illnesses associated with them. The Solar Plexus Center and the Splenic Center are mirrors of each other. There are three awareness centers in the body: the Solar Plexus Center, the Splenic Center, and the Ajna Center. The Solar Plexus Center brings emotionally related illnesses, the Splenic Center brings immune illnesses, and the Ajna Center brings mental illnesses. [This statement has not been validated in scientific or clinical research and is not likely to be valid based on my clinical experience.]

The Generator: An Energy Type

When the Sacral Center is activated by a channel, the person is a Generator (Figure 4). Generators are designed "to wait" and "to respond" to the energy of others. This person's true power comes out of response and is not in words but is rather in the sacral voice, which makes sounds, such as "uh-huh" ("yes") and "un-un" ("no"). For the Generator, it is always most important to be asked.

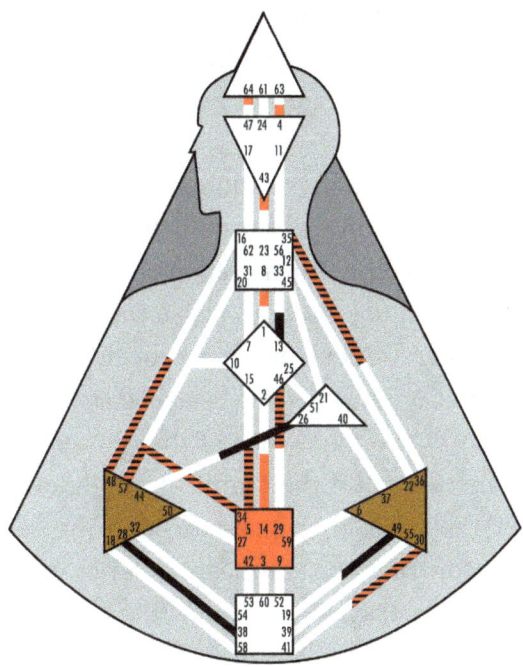

Figure 4: The Generator

A Generator is not designed to take action but rather is designed to wait to respond to others. Their power comes out of that. They must be asked so that they can respond out of their true voice, otherwise, they may be responding incorrectly for themselves. Sacral beings are very powerful, but they also experience deep frustration because we encourage people in our society to manifest, i.e., to take action rather than wait to respond. [Because Generators described in the Human Design System are likely to become Manifesting Generators in their Integrated Human Design, it is important for them to wait to know what they know is right for them and to be clear that when they consider action, it honors their inner alignment. For example, an individual may think something is right for them and when they allow time to pass and they reconsider their options, they may decide to act or to wait. The response can be an internal response or a response to outside stimuli.]

The Generator (Figure 4) responds [from their sacral center.] True Generators are often mistakenly identified as Manifestors. People assume they are a Manifestor because they have a motor center defined as the Throat Center. If the motor center defined to the Throat Center is the Sacral Center, they are Manifestors by definition only.

If the Sacral Center, which is a motor center, is connected to the Throat Center through some other center or directly, that person is a Manifesting Generator. This person is a Manifestor with a special consideration because they are also a Generator. It is also true that the Manifesting Generator (someone whose Sacral Center reaches the Throat Center) needs to be asked so their action occurs in response and has the true voice of that person. The difference between the Generator and the Manifesting Generator is that the Generator that responds then goes through the sacral stages of development. In contrast, the Manifesting Generator who responds can leap right into the fray. [The Manifesting Generator has to wait to know if their considered action is right for them or not. It is always part of the human process to go within and determine what

THE FOUR [FIVE] TYPES

is aligned with you and what is not. Your process does not depend on outside forces. A Manifesting Generator envisions what they want to have happen and then determines if it aligns internally with their inner gut response. I recommend going slow and tuning in to the inner self. When I ran the statistics on 5,000 cases, the data confirmed that there are indeed five Types: the Manifestor, Manifesting Generator, Generator, Projector, and Reflector. These Types are statistically independent of each other.]

Their true strategy in life is the same as the Generator's strategy. They must wait to respond. There is an important difference between the Generator and the Manifesting Generator. The Generator who responds goes through the sacral stages of development, whereas the Manifesting Generator who responds can leap right into the fray.

Response is key. Generators need to be asked. [internally or by an outside source.] But be cognizant of the subtlety of this energy. Questions come in many ways, and as long as the response is from the gut level of the Sacral Center with the true voice of the Sacral being, it is a response. Have you ever experienced a person who eats, and while they do, they respond, "Mmmmmm?" or when someone hugs you, they go, "Hmmmmmm?" These are Sacral beings who are responding. Begin to notice.

Because Generators are here to "respond," they suffer deep frustration when they are not asked for their response or when their response is not acknowledged and, therefore, honored. Because the Generator has the Sacral Center defined, that Center, which functions like a gearbox, tends to get stuck in things. Thus, many Generators suffer frustration because they are stuck in situations or illness or relationships and they are not able to initiate change. Generators are not here to initiate anything, ever. When they do not initiate when they respond, they are entering into things correctly; otherwise, they are entering into things incorrectly, and whatever it is will never be right for them. [We are designed to be whole, integrated beings. Teaching a Generator to self-reflect on what is right for them or not is far more powerful than placing the questioner outside of the self. In fact, in the Kabbalistic Tree of Life, the first Path that we enter as an incarnating soul is through the Sacral Center toward the Root Center. According to the Kabbalistic teachings, the seat of the spirit resides in the Sacral Center, and it is from the Sacral Center we know ourselves to be Divine Beings living in a physical/biological body.]

The Generator responds to illness, but it does not manifest it. When you look at Generators, you are looking at people who get ill from other people. They take it in from the other. The root of the Generator, the Sacral Center, is the life force. Generators are the major potential illness carriers in the world. Because Generators respond, they also respond to illness. [All illness predictions by Ra were not substantiated statistically in the research on 30,000 cases and on another 15,000 clinically.] They do not manifest illness, but they get ill from other people.

Generators operate out of frustration. This is their basic dilemma. Their frustration leads them to be called into and pulled into things, which makes them ill. They are always taking things in from other people and responding to them. [This statement is not true.] In a classroom where the mumps are going around, you will see that all the children with a defined Sacral Center get it first. It may be a Manifestor that generated it originally. Once the illness, however, is there, all the Generators are potential candidates for taking it in. They take it in my response. If the Generator is responding rather than acting out of frustration, this can be a healthy process for the immune system. [None of the statements Ra made attributing illness to various Types or lines held up to statistical scrutiny. Statistics did not show the prevalence of illness related to Type.]

The Generator can take the illness in, and the response of the immune system may defend the Generator against it. A Generator with an open Splenic Center may take in the illness and get ill. This response to illness can be healthy because, through this response, the immune system learns the experience and can defend better afterward.

Any time that you are dealing with people with a defined Sacral Center, you know that they are open to contagion. They are open to things that are going around. They can absorb them easily; they can "pull things in." [This is an erroneous statement.]

Because the Sacral Center is more powerful than the Throat Center, a Manifestor who has a defined Sacral Center is really a Generator. The Sacral Center, whenever defined, means that these are people who are responding. This means that the individual is designed to meet those forces on the other side and respond to them.

When you are dealing with Type, the Generator has to be asked. Ask a Generator, "Do you want to catch a cold? The Generator will answer, "No." *Responding is the whole thing.* When a Generator is not asked, that is when they get sick. It is one of those things to recognize in terms of how you deal with them. Generators have to be asked, "Do you want help?" When a caregiver recognizes how to deal with Generators, i.e., they ask the Generator what they want, and the caregiver waits for the response, the relationship becomes one of greater trust and healing. [These statements are not substantiated clinically or statistically.]

You cannot tell them because if you tell them, "This is what is wrong with you, and you need this and this and this," it does not work. Even though you give them the right medicine, even though they take the right medicine, it is not going to work. You have to ask them, " Do you want me to treat you in this condition?" You have to ask them, "Do you want to take this medicine?"

You have to ask them if they want your help because then when they respond, they take in the positive of that response. This is natural for Generators because their authority comes out of their response. Then you can help them. But you cannot help them by telling them. This is critical! For the best outcome in patient management, ask the patient and the Generator and wait for the response.

If you are a Generator, make sure the people in your life know to ask you what your response is to things. Have them ask you questions so you can know your own response to things. Get into the habit of watching your response and notice how often it is the gut sound of "uh-huh" ("yes") or "un-un" ("no"). When you first recognize this aspect of yourself, it may amuse and surprise you, but then it becomes a reassurance that you are living in a way that is true to your nature. Make sure your care professional is asking you if the treatment is right for you and if you want to take the medicine you are being asked to take. Your response will be key in your healing process. [As a Generator, learn to always check with your inner self to know if your responses honor your inner alignment or not. You are not dependent on outside forces for inner alignment and clarity. You know what you know, and no one can tell you what you do not know. Stand firmly and securely in your knowing.]

In addition, if you are the parent of a Generator child, be aware that your child needs to be asked rather than told to do things. [All children, regardless of Type, should be listened to and asked for confirmation of what is right for them.] Learn to respect that response if you expect your child to develop self-esteem and self-love.

For a Generator, responding is the whole thing. Ask Generators in your life, "Do you want help?" or "Do you want to eat this for dinner?" or "Do you want to play this sport?" When a Generator works, and works correctly, their tendency to overwork and to overdo comes into harmony and balance. [We have no data on this characteristic.] A Generator who is asked for their response works well and happily. They feel their own life force power, and they experience it; it is, then, that out of their response, the life force power can be shared and of use to others in their life and work. Otherwise, the Generator is unhappy and feels stuck; the life force energy becomes degenerative instead of generative.

The moment you ask a Generator, and they respond, they take

in the positive of that response. This is natural for Generators because their authority comes out of their response. [A Generator is capable of inner questioning and inner alignment of what is right for them or not. Even a young baby responds according to what is right for them. Responding in alignment with our deep spiritual self is innate and resistant to challenges.]

The Non-Energy Types: The Projector and The Reflector

The Projector

A Projector (Figure 5) is a person who has a connected channel in their Design, but that channel is not connected either to a Motor (fuel) Center that reaches the Throat Center or to the Sacral Center.

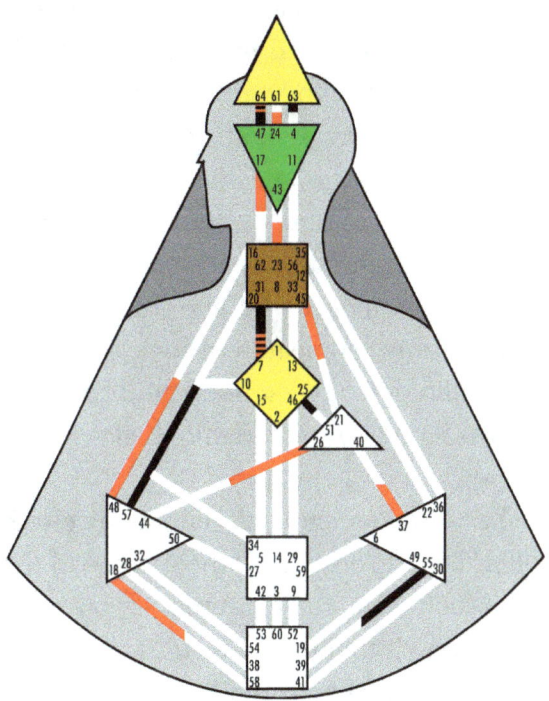

Figure 5: The Projector

This person is someone who, because they are not designed to take action and do not necessarily know their gut-level response, is here to be recognized by others. [As long as a Projector takes time to go within and knows what aligns energetically with their core self, they do not need to check with someone else to gain clarity. This strategy has been tested in my clinical practice.] Projectors may have numerous open Centers or be defined in numerous Centers. Their sensitivity is acute, and often, they are not recognized for who they really are. [Open Centers open a person to all energy cosmically impacting them, and thus, they have the capacity to make choices that are in the now and that align with them in their present situation.]

In a Projector, the channel or channels that are defined reveal the qualities and strengths of the person. It is this nature that needs to be recognized in order for the Projector to feel the power of being who they are and to be able to experience that power in the world. Because of their nature, Projectors hunger for energy release or access through being recognized by others. [This statement does not hold up clinically.] In a body graph, there are actually more projector channels of energy than any other channel. In addition, all of the mental system [Ra is specifically referring to the Crown and Ajna Centers as the mental system.] is made up of projected channels. Thus, by understanding Projectors and their nature and Type, you begin to understand and know why recognition is so important to so many people and in society. [Self-recognition is more important than outer recognition. Thus, when we point out how energy operates and how to tap into the various channels and centers, we empower our clients.]

A Projector has to be recognized. Somebody else has to recognize the problem for a Projector. Someone has to tell a Projector that they do not look well. For example, if you have a Projector child, you have to watch that child like a hawk. That child will not independently recognize when something is wrong with them. It is so simple. It would not be true if it was not simple.

THE FOUR [FIVE] TYPES

An important thing to always remember in looking at a body graph is that the areas and centers that are not colored in are not broken; they do not need to be fixed in any way. They are very important in a person's Design because they are where that person learns [and where they have freedom of choice with no predisposing tendencies.] It is where they gain wisdom in their life. It is through these undefined centers that we are conditioned [conditioning is a very specific psychological term and is misleading here.] We are vulnerable to the energy of others and the transits (the movement of the Planets). In Design, wisdom is always the potential in what you do not have, the gate you do not have, the center that's undefined, whatever the case may be.

A Projector has areas of their Design that are uncolored. They are very sensitive to the auras and energies of those around them for that reason. [Ideally,] the Projector has learned through their contact with different energy Types and different energy configurations how those different energies affect them. The Projector knows those centers where they have definitions. That is what they're here to be wise about. In the moment that Projectors stop identifying with their undefined Centers they become aware of themselves in a new way. They have real wisdom then about their capacity to be conditioned. [Influenced is a more accurate word than conditioned] by others' energies. [We need to validate this with more research, but it seems valid from my clinical research.]

Projectors need a formal invitation to allow their energy to come out; they need to be recognized for their ability and their capacity. [Recognition may come from outside a Projector or from the Projector's internal responses.] Once they are recognized, they have the energy to be successful with that aspect of themselves because others have recognized that aspect of their life. Think how important that is for a child. A parent who recognizes their Projector child for the talents and other qualities that the child has enables the child's capacity to express those aspects of itself and to shine. A parent who denies that to/of the Projector child denies the child the possibility of early realization of its full potential. This statement about recognition applies to all Types and all children. Because so many channels are Projector channels, most people have aspects that are Projector aspects. A person, for example, who has a Projector channel may need to be recognized for their specific talent or their storytelling ability, and those qualities may need to be noticed and encouraged by another person before those qualities will be visible or recognized by the person himself. As a child develops input from outside authorities, the input impacts their self-esteem. It is natural for all Types to benefit from empowering support and to turn away from support that undermines their self-esteem.

The Manifestor has anger, the Generator has frustration, and the Projector has bitterness. The Projector gets all this sour stuff in their process. This is where they feel it. Everything can really go sour for a Projector: their blood, their flesh, and their stomach. [These labels of feelings attributed to different Types do not hold up clinically.]

The Projector literally stands around and waits. You have to recognize them and then invite them to care. You can tell them. You can say, "I see very clearly that you have a problem," because that is essential. The next step is, "I would like to be able to help you." Invite Projectors into well-being. Unlike with a Generator, if you ask a Projector if they want help, it does not mean anything to them. What a Projector needs and wants must be seen. Someone else has to recognize the need or want in them. [There is no validity in this statement.] They trust you only when they know that you see and know who they are in their strengths and weaknesses. [All Types want to be recognized for who they are and how they respond. Everyone wants recognition and support at the core of their being.] They trust you because you recognize them and because you recognize their problems. Once trust exists, the Projector can be invited into healing. Projectors must be invited to be helped. [An aware Projector can look inward to know what they need.]

A Projector cannot insist on recognition because they do not get it that way. Projectors can only take in those who truly, spontaneously recognize them, otherwise the relationship does not work for them. Moreover, because Projectors are so sensitive and open to the environment and to others, a healing environment is essential for them. Timing of things is also crucial for the Projector. As you become familiar with how Transits of the Planets work, you will note that certain potentials in channels get "hooked up" at different times. For a Projector, such a connection may make an enormous difference in their energy, healing, and well-being. [Most Projectors become Manifesting Generators in the Integrated Charts.]

Because Projectors do not always recognize things in themselves, they need to have regular check-ups so that things that may be amiss can be diagnosed early. In addition, parents, relatives, and friends of Projectors need to pay attention to the Projector and recognize and acknowledge their perceptions of the Projector. Such recognition is extremely important to the Projector. [We cannot verify this at this time.]

Manifestors and Generators have different healing processes than the Projectors and Reflectors. They can heal more quickly because they have energy systems built into them that are constantly at work. When dealing with a Projector, it does not necessarily work that way. Because the Projector does not have its energy system built into it, a healing environment is essential for it.

The timing for taking medicines is essential for Projectors who have an undefined Splenic Center. When they take a medicine into their body, it has to be able to be processed through their splenic system. When a Projector who lives alone, who has an undefined Splenic Center, takes a medicine, there is absolutely no guarantee that it is going to work for them, even if it is the perfect medicine. It gets stuck, and it will not be able to move through their system. [There is no evidence that this statement is true.]

What happens often for these people is that they take a medicine, and even though it is the correct medicine, they leave their doctor. They go to another doctor, and they get some other medicine. It so happens that there is a transit that week that allows the new medicine to go to the spleen. Even though they were given not the best medicine, and even though they may not be dealing with the best doctor, the timing is now right. The Projector ends up thinking their healing is all about the doctor.

This phenomenon can also lead to problems. Many Projectors are subject to transit delusion. They take medicine when there is time through transit, and they really think it is the medicine and the person who gave it to them.

It is the same thing with psychotherapy. You may be dealing with someone who has poor self-esteem, and you want them to have willpower. A therapist who has a defined Heart Center pumps them up and says they have to be willful. [A competent clinician would handle a client with poor self-esteem gently and would not tell their client to be willful. Therapists elicit motivation and goals from their clients and do not attempt to change their innate internal patterns that make them who they are.] If there happens to be a transit that hooks up their Heart Center for a week or a month, they are going to think that therapist is the best therapist that ever lived. Only when that transit goes away do they go back to their own nature, and they discover that their willfulness has actually made them sick. Then they are going to say, "That was not good; I'll have to try another one."

Timing becomes essential. Whenever you look at a non-energy Type, you always have to see that timing is everything for them. [Who a non-energy Type comes in contact with is important since anyone with an open Center picks up energy frequencies of those people and animals in their presence as well as the collective energy.] Also, they do not recognize things outside of themselves, e.g., that they are sitting beside somebody who has a cold. They get a lot of things. They need to be recognized, yet they do not recognize themselves. It is an interesting mirror of their Type. [Recognizing Type and energy sensitivity can be taught and monitored.]

A Projector without motors will not recognize when physical activity is detrimental rather than positive. They have no way of judging that. They are not an energy Type, and they do not recognize these things. They push their body. It is typical of Projectors. By not having any motors, energy and power sports are enormously attractive to them. Projectors often do well with group sports for this reason; they are open to the energies of those in the team or group and thrive on using that energy to excel. The more open the Projector is, the more attractive these things become.

The fact that so much is open in a Projector also means that the Projector can be very skillful in recognizing a good athlete from a bad athlete. A Projector can even learn and develop all those skills themselves. At the same time, it is not the Projector; it is where the Projector's wisdom is. Wherever the Projector is not defined is where they can become wise. Open centers give people the potential for authority. When a Projector wants to become an athlete and initiates becoming an athlete, they put themselves under enormous stress. *A Projector must always be recognized or invited to show who they are.*

> In my clinical practice, when a Projector is in touch with their core Self, their awareness of what they feel and want is recognized internally, and then as they become a Manifesting Generator through transit or in their Integrated Noble Energy Maps®, they can know what is right for them and to act on it.

How a caregiver structures care for people is very important. The Projector, the non-energy Types, have to have regular visits in order to catch developing illnesses. It is up to the doctor to recognize that there is something wrong with them and so that things that may be amiss can be diagnosed early. A yearly checkup is too much space. Quarterly would work better. They can come by for a 10-minute visit just to be looked at. Just by looking at a Projector every three months, a doctor can see immediately if there is a difference in that person. [There is no data on this point, and the Doctor's sensitivity would be what makes the difference.]

In addition, parents, relatives, and friends of Projectors need to pay attention to the Projector and recognize and acknowledge their perceptions of the Projector. Such recognition is extremely important to the Projector. [We cannot verify this at this time.]

You will mostly encounter the Manifestor, Generator, and Projector Types. Most of your clients/patients will be Generators and Projectors. Manifestors rarely come into the office to ask for help, while reflectors are a less frequently occurring Type. [Neither Marvin nor I have found the clinical data supporting this hypothesis.]

Pediatricians, especially, need this knowledge. It is absolutely essential for keeping children healthy. Pediatricians can learn how to guide the child to be healthy. They can talk to the parents of Projector children and tell them that they have to watch their children. Parents must recognize illness in their child and not rely on or wait for the Projector child to communicate about their illness.

If each of these three Types is living out their nature, if they are living out their Type, they are not going to need the kind of care that other people need. Other people who get sick are overwhelmed because it is the not-self that is getting sick. [This hypothesis is not substantiated.]

The Reflector

A reflector (Figure 6) is a person who has no defined channels in their Design. They are here to reflect energies. They are totally vulnerable in the sense that every one of their centers is open. As a Type, Reflectors are not frequently seen, i.e., they are a rare Type. [0.9% are Reflectors] Reflectors can be quite powerful, but they can also suffer from confused energy. They can get overwhelmed.

> A Reflector has open centers, meaning they are highly sensitive and have choices about what aligns with them and what does not. A Reflector picks up the energy around them and can be

THE FOUR [FIVE] TYPES

confused about what belongs to them and what does not. Inner alignment and self-knowledge are especially important for a Reflector.

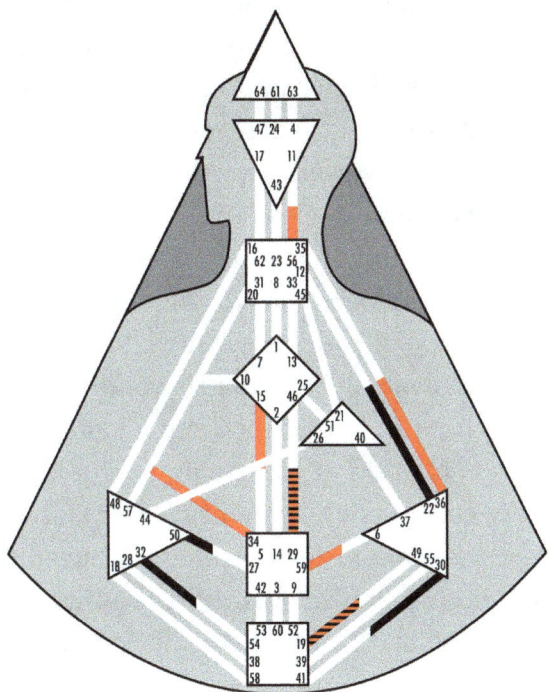

Figure 6: The Reflector

Reflectors look vulnerable, but they are not. They come into the world open. The moment they come into the world, they deal with taking in the auras of others. However, they can get totally drained in that process. Then, they become susceptible to anything because of exhaustion. They are very confused about their own bodies. These are people who, like Projectors, always have to go to others to find out about their own bodies and to find out about their own care. [In my experience clinically, once a Reflector recognizes that they are empathic and need to discern what energies align with them and what does not align with them, they come into their full power and are extremely perceptive. When they understand how to use energy, especially in the Four Worlds, they avoid incoming energy from depleting them. Reflectors who receive guidance on energy sensitivity evolve and can master their sensitivities and use them constructively.]

The Reflector is a Lunar Type. Because of their openness, the Moon creates a pattern for them every 28 days. This pattern activates different aspects of their nature, so they are basically on a 28-day cycle. A Reflector who gets involved in something has to go through the whole 28-day cycle. Even something like a cold may take the Reflector 28 days to clear from their body. [Everyone on Earth experiences the Lunar cycle and is impacted by it.]

If you are a Reflector, know that you are open and vulnerable to the energies around you. You are sensitive to people, places, and things. You are not those things; you respond to them and experience them. You are here to reflect them to others. It is your gift, and it is the lesson to learn. If you are in touch with this aspect of yourself, you are empowered. If you are trying to live who you are not, to be other than you are, you will experience overwhelming exhaustion and confusion. [Any of the Types living out of alignment will be overwhelmed, exhausted, and confused.]

The strength of a Reflector is in the awareness of their openness because then they reflect their true nature rather than trying to live as one of the other Types. The difficulty for a Reflector is that conditioning begins so early in our society, and the Reflector is so open and vulnerable to conditioning. [I think in this instance, Ra was using the term conditioning for socialization. There is a big difference between the two. There are many different kinds of psychological conditioning. What I see clinically is that most individuals resist conditioning and instead hold on to who they know themselves to be regardless of the pain it causes them. In 50 plus years of clinical work, I can document that all my clients were fighting to manifest their true selves. What Ra was actually discussing is socialization which refers to how an individual adapts to the expectations of the culture they live in. This adaptation can occur without compromising the inner Self and its integrity.]

People who change and who do not act consistently day to day, week to week, are often told that there is something wrong with them. Children who change from day to day are told that they need to be different. If you or your child is a Reflector, let yourself reflect on what is around you and begin to see that the strength of your being is in tuning in to the energies and the aura of others and having that experience. Remember that we learn and become wise in those centers that are undefined in our being. Thus, the Reflector is open to great lessons and learning from all the things met in life. To hinder this person from those experiences and to censor them in a certain way is to prevent the open joy that can be there for the Reflector.

The Reflector can also be a great teacher and communicator because the Reflector can mirror the energies of a group or individual. In the positive this person can shine the light on those who they reflect as much as for themselves.

Since Reflectors are the least frequently seen Type [0.9% are Reflectors], when and if you do see a Reflector, realize that they basically do not know their own body. That is the biggest work with them. A Reflector child must be taught about their body. They have to learn how to take care of their body. Because they take in all kinds of different energies and different Types into their process, they have a different challenge than the other Types. Anyone who is so absorbent is always open to taking in all kinds of things from others. [This is accurately stated by Ra. Reflectors are natural empaths and need to learn what is their energy and what is not.]

> Most Reflectors become Manifesting Generators in the Integrated Noble Energy Maps®. Thus, knowing which World and where you are open to picking up energy from others and where you are strongly defined can be empowering. No single Type other than the Manifesting Generator Type is prevalent in the population in terms of how we function as humans.

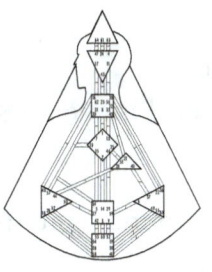

The Nine Centers

By seeing the Types, you can see how illness emerges, whether it bursts out, or whether it is a response. The next step is to look at how and where disease enters the body. It can be seen in undefined Centers. [Statistical analysis showed that defined or undefined Centers did not correlate at all with the occurrence of specific diseases. There was no difference in heart attack patient mortality in a sample of 5000 cases that analyzed those with a defined Heart Center and those with an undefined Heart Center. In general, statistics on 30,000 cases of matched samples did not show that Centers, Gates, or Lines were predictive of any diseases hypothesized by Ra in association with specific Centers, Gates, or Lines.]

Centers Overview

The Nine Centers shown in the Body Graph (Figure 7) describe energy centers, each functioning in its own way, contributing to the configuration of who you are. There are:

4 Motor Centers (Fuel)
- The Root Center
- The Sacral Center

- The Heart Center (Ego)*
- The Solar Plexus Center (Emotional System)**

3 Awareness Centers
- The Splenic Center (Immune System),
- The Ajna Center (Mind)
- The Solar Plexus Center (Emotional System)**

Note that The Solar Plexus Center (Emotional System) is both a Motor (Fuel) Center and an Awareness Center.
**Calling the Heart Center the Ego center is misleading from a psychological perspective*

3 Other Centers
- The Throat Center
- The G Center (Identity, Self)
- The Head Center

Body Graph

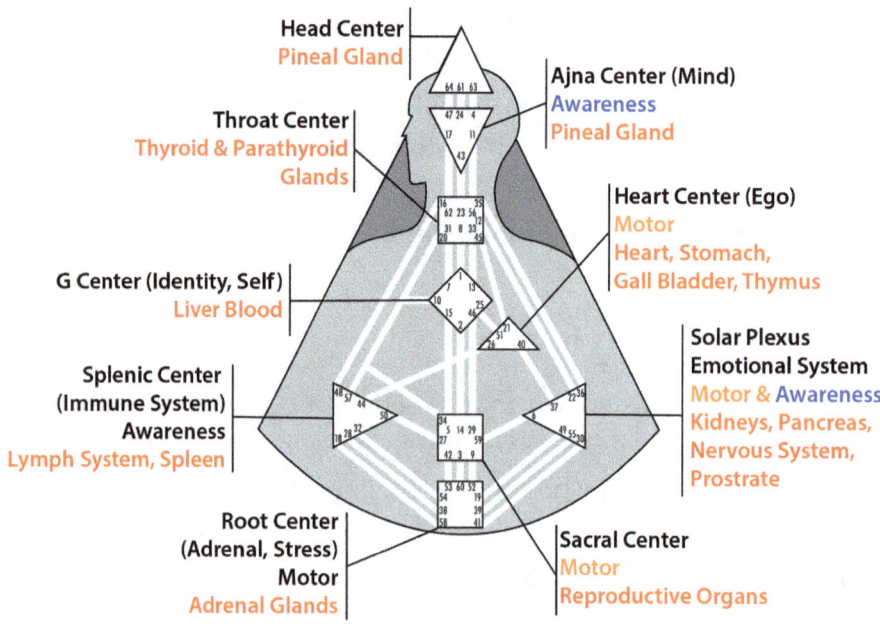

Figure 7: The Centers Labeled

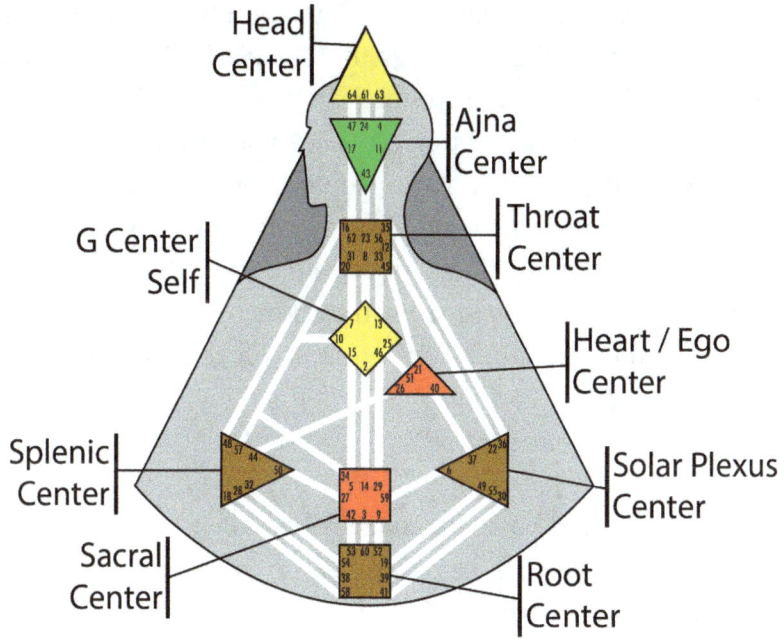

Figure 8: The 9 Centers

In the body graph, each one of the Nine Centers represented has either an endocrine gland or biological organs related to it. Centers are considered defined when there is activation of a Gate on either end of a Channel which connects one Center to another Center.

Activations may be conscious or unconscious. The activations colored into the body graph in black represent the Personality, those energies in ourselves to which we have conscious access. We know and can recognize these energies. They are above ground, so to speak. The activations colored into the body graph in red represent the Design of a person, those energies in ourselves to which we have no conscious access. We are not aware of the functioning of these energies because they are essentially underground, under the surface.

A Center is considered undefined when no Channel connected to it has a definition. In an undefined Center, there may be Gates that are active but which do not connect to the Gate on the other side of that Channel. When this configuration happens, the active Gate acts as a potential of energy that is always there and which seeks its completion on the other side of the Channel.

When you have an activation and seek its other side, you might have repeated interactions with people who have that Gate, and they may seem familiar to you because they represent an energy that you have met many times in your life. Through a basic understanding of Centers and their role in your own Design, you begin to see, know, and understand how people affect you when they enter your space (aura). [A channel may be defined in one World and not in another, and a Channel may be activated by a Gate activation in another World.]

You now have the basic language necessary to understand the body graph and its colors. Layer upon layer is possible in Design. It is a treasure map with breadth and depth. This brief introductory lesson is for the purpose of giving you the language and the taste of what is possible through self-knowledge.

Simple, practical, and do it yourself; you do not need many books, many tapes, or any gurus or therapists. You need your own knowledge of your type and the willingness to experiment with living who you are. By doing this experiment, doors open, and you walk forward into the true adventure of life itself. [Statistics show that 33.5% of the population are Manifesting Generators in their Mental/Waking World, or their basic Human Design, while more than 95% of the population are Manifesting Generators in their Integrated Human Design (Noble Energy Maps®, the design body map that includes how they function in all worlds.]

The Head Center

The Head Center (Figure 9) relates to the pineal gland. Although the pineal gland is not yet fully understood scientifically, it seems likely that its main function is to move neurotransmitters from the grey areas of the brain to the frontal lobes. It is a border guard. [We now know that the pineal gland produces melatonin, a serotonin-derived hormone that modulates sleep patterns following the diurnal cycles.]

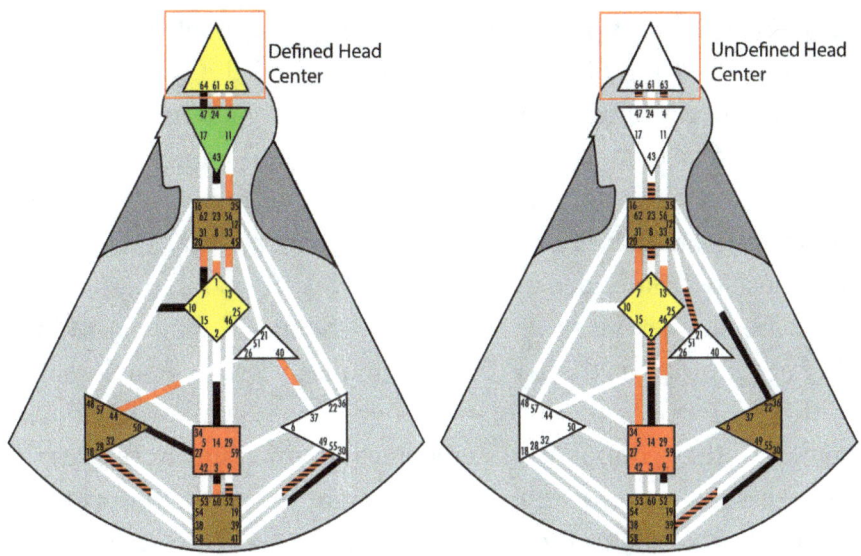

Figure 9: The Head Center

The Head Center and the Root Center are the sources of all stress and pressure in life! Three Formats have parallel structures in both the Head Center and the Root Center. These formats are Abstract, Individual, and Logical. They will be discussed in more detail in the section on The Root Center. This fact is very important to understand. Someone with an undefined Head Center and an undefined Root Center is always caught in life's sandwich. This sandwich is necessary. The pressure is there in order to move the life process. [Ra correctly referred to the way we receive divine energy through our Crown Center and ground ourselves through our feet.] Life can be full of pressure and stress. [When you have an undefined Center, you are dealing with something that magnifies whatever moves through it. If you have an undefined Center, you are empathically sensitive to all energy possibilities aligned with the Center's function. You may pick up energy from those people and situations you are exposed to.]

Someone with an undefined Head Center is someone whose head hurts them a lot. [I have not found this statement to hold up clinically in my research on 15,000 cases.] Look at someone who has the Gate of Confusion (Gate 64) and the Gate of Doubt (Gate 63) in an undefined Head Center. They go along, and there is no mind because it is undefined. Someone comes along and hooks up that Head Center. The moment that happens, the Head Center reflects that energy twice as strongly as what connects it, and those two Gates are instantly activated. [Ra's statement is true for some people, but not everyone experiences it that way.] When they become active, there is this enormous pressure to make sense of things. There is this enormous pressure to come up with the answer. If they cannot, what happens to them is slowly, but surely, the pressure becomes a permanent state in them. The pressure begins to overwhelm them. [A more empowering way to describe what Ra was implying is that when a Channel hooks up, you feel the energy of it, and if the connection is in the Crown to Ajna Centers, it becomes a focus in your mind. Depending on your nature, you may feel pressure or you may feel inspired, excited, or creative. Consider how you experience each Channel when it activates in you. Each individual is unique.]

What comes out of that is a number of things. The first signs are sleep disturbance and mental fatigue. This is the first sign that something is wrong with the way the Head Center operates. It is not about having the occasional nightmare because that is normal.

We already know that people with Fibromyalgia tend to have undefined Head and Ajna Centers and that they are prone to sleep disturbances. [The statistical data do not support this statement about fibromyalgia patients.] We also know that they are highly hypnotizable. [Fibromyalgia patients are, in fact, highly hypnotizable.] Putting this information together with design information is a very important process because it confirms the importance of the Head Center as a neurotransmitter reservoir. In our Head Center, we try to make sense out of things. We have pressure there to understand and comprehend the world and its ideas.

Those people who have a defined Head Center often are people who have many thoughts and ideas, in which they are fixed. People with undefined Head Centers tend to be open to many ideas, but the pressure in their Head Centers may also make them prone to Headaches. [The statistical data on 30,000 people and on 15,000 clinical cases does not support that people with an undefined Head Center are more prone to headaches.] They are people who try to solve their lives through their minds. They would never get headaches if they did not give their mind authority. Nobody's mind can ever dictate what is right or wrong for them in this life.

Anxiety in the Head Center is very different from anxiety in the Ajna Center. The awareness centers all carry fear. The Splenic Center (immune system) deals with the very basic fear of survival. The Ajna Center deals with fear as anxiety and mental anxiety. The Solar Plexus Center deals with nervousness. Physical nervousness comes out of the Solar Plexus Center. [These statements are erroneous. The Crown and Ajna Centers operate to focus our Minds on issues of the moment, especially in the Mental and Emotional Worlds. Emotional Reactivity in the Solar Plexus Center must be transformed through the Emotional/Angelic World 33-Gate Matrix. Focusing the Mind does not always carry anxiety or fear. It can be highly exciting and creative. Consider each of these health statements based on your experiences, and do not take Ra's proclamation as fact in this area.]

The Head Center is an inspiration field and a pressure field. With an undefined Head Center, a person gets a headache because they try to solve their life through their mind. They would never get headaches if they did not give their mind authority. Nobody's mind can ever dictate what is right or wrong for them in this life.

Many people with an open Head Center suffer horrible pain in their head because they try to figure out with their head what to do. They get to the point where the pressure in their head is overwhelming. They beat their head against the wall; they take pain relievers, aspirin, etc. Their mind tries to claim authority. At the mundane level, this causes headaches.

> When looking at the body map, consider what Channels and Gates are active and read the description of that Channel and/or Gate in its specific World. If you are working with a client, ask your client about their experience instead of giving them input that may not be accurate. When you are reading a chart, you are giving someone input on the spiritual dimension. Thus, your language and input are taken in on an unconscious level and can disempower them if you use words that may not be empowering. A word like pressure or headache can be detrimental because it can take root and disempower the unconscious of your client and may activate a headache or pressure by its very suggestion. If you are coaching or doing readings, learn to use Clean Language and skills appropriate for each World.

A Manifestor who lives like that may end up with a brain tumor, a blood clot in the brain, or a stroke. [This statement has no basis in fact.] They can end up with all kinds of things that get to the extreme at some point. Extremes happen, particularly with hot Types, whether it is the Manifestor Type or the Generator Type, because of their energy power. In their anger and frustration of not being able to have their mind guide their life, the Head Center of theirs begins to implode. Alzheimer's disease and the loss of memory are rooted in improper operation of the Head Center. If the Head Center operates improperly, then the stored memory is not being properly processed, and that can lead to all kinds of deterioration. Parkinson's is similar in that sense. [We now know that Parkinson's disease relates to issues related to genetics, toxins, and the gut, not to a defined or undefined Head Center.]

In almost 90 percent of cases of illness, the illness comes in through undefined motors. The motors are so powerful. If you are not equipped for them and you actually try to live them out as if they are your own, you really get negative conditioning there. [Learning how to manage undefined Centers is important for your quality of life but does not correlate statistically with diseases.]

The Ajna Center

The Ajna Center (Figure 10) is different. With the Ajna Center, you are dealing with the pituitary gland. The lobes of the pituitary gland, both the anterior and posterior lobes, are very powerful. They are the command posts for most of our endocrine functions. They are at the top of the food chain in the endocrine system. The Ajna Center deals with anxiety as a theme. [A better description of the theme of the Ajna Center would be focus and truth. In my clinical work, individuals with a defined Ajna Center generally know what others are thinking, so they are telepathically attuned to others. In addition, they focus on issues of concern to them and stay with them until they find a resolution that aligns with their values. Remember, the Crown and Ajna are in the Mental/Waking and Emotional/Angelic Worlds. In the Emotional/Angelic World, the Head Centers relate to the Creative Intelligence that is thinking that includes compassion for others and tunes in to the Collective Consciousness of knowledge. These Worlds aim to find a path of optimal functioning in your culture and your reality World. Within the Head Centers are at least eight hormones directly affecting organ function or "tropic" hormones that stimulate distant endocrine glands.]

HUMAN DESIGN & HEALTH

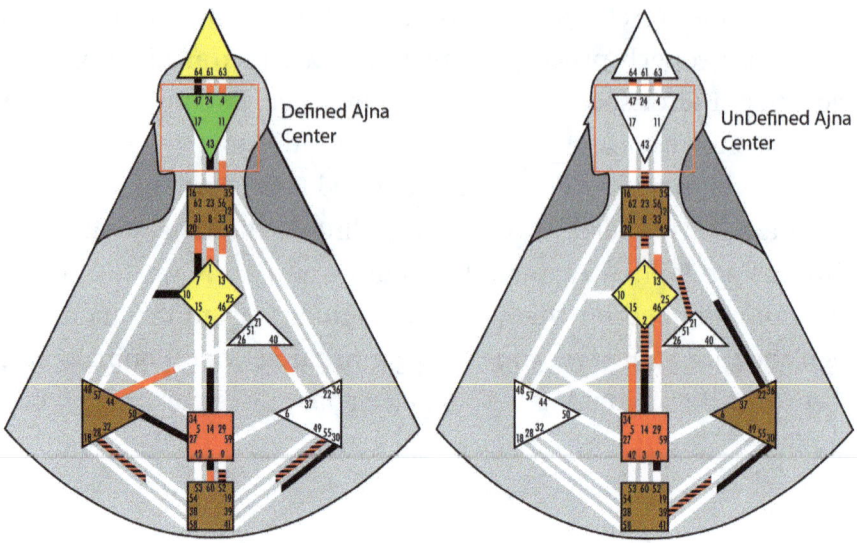

Figure 10: The Ajna Center

When you are dealing with a person who has an undefined Ajna Center, you can know right away that you are dealing with anxiety. The anxiety, depending on the nature of their circuitry, is,

- "Can I make myself understood?"
- "Can I explain myself?"
- "Can I make sense out of myself?"
- "Can I make sense out of my life?"

Generally, people with an undefined Ajna Center have eye problems. The 17th Gate is the right eye; the 11th Gate is the left eye. An eye problem is the deterioration of vision based on not being able to have one's mind do what it wants to do. Slowly, the eyes stop being able to see properly. This can also be true for someone who has a defined Ajna Center. [There is no data to support this statement.]

By not living out their Type, a person who gives their mind mental authority at the level of the Ajna Center is trying to overcome anxiety. Still, they actually create more anxiety for themselves. The

Ajna Center is not about biological illness at the mental level that is found in the Head Center, where there is pressure. The Head Center is where the physical problems, the physical headaches, and the physical disease have their basis.

In the Ajna Center are mental diseases. There, anxiety can become neurosis; anxiety can lead to all kinds of things. Out of that, people end up getting into things that can make them ill, but it is important to see that there are two mental Centers that operate in physically different ways. [Interpret Ra's statements about anxiety and illness carefully. Stay focused on the Channels and the Gates, along with their meaning in the Kabbalistic Tree of Life and their astrological nuances. You will find more empowerment and meaning for your clients in doing it this way.]

In the Ajna Center (Mind), there are the anxiety fears - the mental anxiety of not being able to communicate. It is the fear of not being understood or the fear that somebody will know or make sense of what is being delivered. The anxiety is about the capacity to be able to communicate with clarity. If clear communication fails, then anxiety surfaces and leads to problems. [No clinical or statistical evidence indicates more anxiety in people with either a defined or an open Ajna Center. Channels defined or undefined give nuance to the energy of the Center, and we have no data linking anxiety to the Ajna Center.]

The Head Center has its impact at the physical level. The Ajna Center (Mind) is experienced as anxiety. In the case of the Ajna Center (Mind), it does not make any difference whether the Center is open or defined. The mental plane is so powerful for us that it is often given Authority in our lives when it never, in fact, has inner Authority.

All of us, from the moment we come into the world, try to organize our world through that mental facility. No Ajna Center (Mind), defined or undefined, ever has inner Authority. Anyone who has a defined Ajna Center determined to live life and do things the way their mind wants ends up suffering from anxiety.

Only when we change primary education can we change the way in which we are brought into the World. Instead of being told it is up to us, we can see that it is not up to us. In that, the most important thing is the way in which the mind works. Minds have outer authority over others. The mind has no inner authority ever. The mind has value for others but absolutely no reliable decision-making value for oneself.

> The Crown and the Ajna Centers operate primarily in the Mental/Waking and the Emotional/Angelic Worlds. While the mind does not have authority over our life processes, we do use our mind to shift energy and think through what we value and want to orchestrate in our lives. Emotional reactivity operates only in the Mental World. Using the mind to transform emotionality into a higher frequency is a crucial function of the mind.

The Throat Center

The Throat Center (Figure 11) is really at the Center of what it is to be human. All of us are here to manifest as a species.

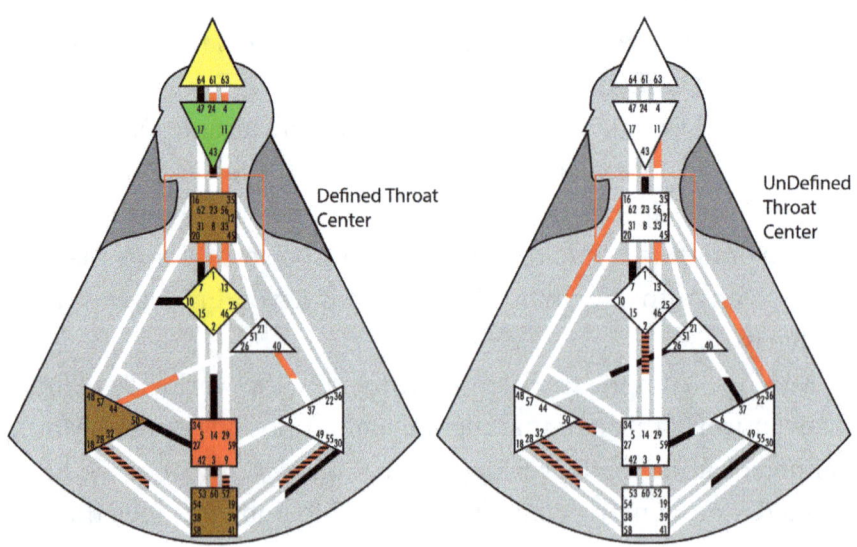

Figure 11: The Throat Center

Because in our society, we put so much emphasis on "doing," and because not everyone is designed "to do," there is enormous pressure on the Throat Center. Both the Thyroid gland and the Parathyroid gland are in the Throat Center. Metamorphosis and metabolism are in the Throat Center. Thyroid damage is one of the most common problems.

A malfunctioning thyroid causes most obesity. [Most obesity is related to the gut flora, not to the thyroid gland.] The Thyroid Gland malfunctions because people are not living out their nature. An abused or misused Thyroid Gland breaks down very quickly. With less than 15% of the population being true Manifestors and Americans being conditioned to Manifest and valued for Manifesting, Throat Center issues are very common. They point to the seriousness of not honoring the true nature of ourselves. Note that the Throat Center is the most complex Center with eleven Gates. [Ra's statements on the etiology of thyroid problems are unsubstantiated. Neither Thyroid issues nor weight gain have been documented as related to a defined or undefined Throat Center.]

An undefined Throat Center is very potent. It indicates that the whole metabolic process is being conditioned by outside forces. Whenever you have somebody who tries to be a Manifestor and has an undefined Throat Center, the thyroid automatically suffers damage. It happens quickly, and it can cause terrible suffering. [Many people with an open Throat Center do not suffer from thyroid issues. Any disease is likely to have multiple etiologies. As in most physical issues, diseases are multifactorial and may be activated by genetics, diet, toxins, stress, and the gut biome. Thus, it is wise to ask your clients about their experience with an open as compared to a defined Center, rather than making any assumptions medically. Remember that when doing a reading on someone, you are in an authority position, and your language and suggestions carry weight and power. Use your words carefully and err on the side of empowering your clients.]

These problems can be seen in the body as well as in the Throat

Center. Locomotive problems, i.e., the way in which the body moves, can be one of the expressions of Throat Center problems. For a person with an undefined Throat Center, manifesting is something that is conditioned. The way these people express themselves through their bodies is conditioned by those around them, and it is not consistent. They end up putting enormous stress on their body, which is not designed to handle that stress. On a physical level, many people with undefined Throat Centers have posture problems; they always call for a chiropractor. They always seem to have a physical problem that needs adjusting on the physical level.

Because of the pressure on the Throat Center, a person with an undefined Throat Center, who is not living out their Type, cannot process energy properly. They end up storing and unloading a lot of things. They can end up with radical weight loss. Normally, however, what happens is they gain a lot of weight. [This statement is unsubstantiated.]

A person with a defined Throat Center that is cut off is even more powerful than a person with an undefined Throat Center. People with a defined Throat Center that is cut off have metabolisms that do not work consistently so they end up putting on a lot of weight; this weight gain is normal for them, in that sense. [There is no validity in this statement.]

By knowing your Design and the Design of people close to you, you can help relieve many of the pressures put upon these people to be other than who they are designed to be. If you have a child, for example, who is a Generator, that child, when pushed to initiate action, will have enormous stress on their thyroid and their Throat Center. If you have a child who is a Manifestor, on the other hand, that child is designed to initiate and act and is not someone who wants to be asked or who wants to ask permission to do things. The pressure on the Throat Center of a Manifestor comes from the resistance they face when asked to "not" manifest as they are designed "to do." [Consider the whole design in its multidimensional perspective before making assumptions about how someone functions. Ask your clients about patterns of behavior and stress before making any assumptions about the impact on their health and psychological well-being.]

Also, when the Throat Center is undefined, the person can speak in many voices, and the Throat Center may reflect who is in their aura. So, someone of this nature is not "changing what they say" to be difficult or because they did not mean what they said before; they are just reflecting their Throat Center, the voice, of the person they are with. We are designed to be as we are, not different. It is important to respect that in each other and in ourselves. [Thus, if you have an open Center, you pick up energy from other people and situations you are in and may or may not know that you are responding to incoming energy that impacts you. Be aware if you have an open Center that you are empathic and take that into account before speaking or acting.]

A person with a defined Throat Center can always speak. The pressure is on the Throat Center to speak and express. Asking a person not to speak makes it very difficult for that person. In fact, a person with a defined Throat Center may sometimes speak or act without knowing why. [This statement is unsubstantiated.]

Allergies seem to be related to not "speaking or manifesting" in our own voice, i.e., in the voice we are designed to use. [This statement is erroneous.] Thus, acceptance of the "proper" voices in ourselves or in the other person for being who we are designed to be is extremely loving and validating of our nature. Furthermore, when we honor our true nature, we can be healthy.

> The Throat Center is a very important Center because of its eleven Gates and, thus, eleven Channels that connect from it. The Throat Center is our center for communication through language, and it also relates to breathing, swallowing, and speaking at the same time. There are different voices associated with each Gate in the Throat Center.

The G Center / Self

The G Center (Self) (Figure 12) is the liver, the center of identity for us in our body. This Center is very important because it is a center of who we are and also because, medically, it corresponds to the liver. The liver is the organ in the body that is responsible for clearing out toxins and which is essential for processing the absorbed nutrients that we process for survival. The liver is also a storage organ; it helps with absorption as well as immunity. The liver "bud" is formed very early in fetal development.

The liver is an extremely important life-essential organ whose functions include:

- Producing and modifying proteins, fats, and carbohydrates; steroid hormones; antibodies; bile that aids in absorption.
- Modifying eternal substances, e.g., detoxifying the body from environmental pollutants and the effects of ingested pre-scribed drugs or other toxic substances.

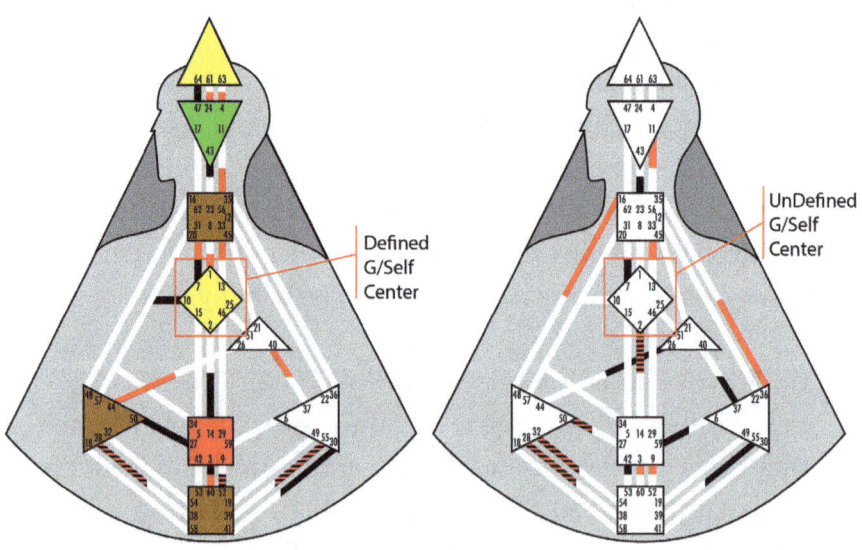

Figure 12: The G or Self Center

People with undefined G Centers (Self) who are really lost in terms of their identity often have liver problems. Deterioration in the liver is very serious because the liver has many cells that cannot be replaced and that are critical for the health of the body. [These statements by Ra are unsubstantiated. I believe that the Self Center is more likely the lungs. Since Channel 45-21 is the only Channel in the body map connecting directly from the Throat Center to the heart muscle itself, it makes sense that it is the primary oxygen transporter to the body. The heart pumps oxygenated blood to the rest of the body through the lungs. Channel 51/25 is the Channel through which the oxygenated blood circulates to the lungs and then from there to the rest of the body. It is possible that the Self Center also includes the liver, but there is no one-to-one correspondence between the organs in the body and the body map.]

The liver is the organ in the body that is responsible for clearing out toxins and which is essential for processing many of the fats and chemicals that we process for survival. The liver is also a storage organ; it helps with absorption as well as immunity. The liver is developed in the fetus very early in development.

If someone has an undefined G Center (Self), they end up being initiated (brought) into sickness. Someone says to them, "Let's go out tonight and go swimming," and they get initiated into getting ill. For people with an undefined G Center (Self), if they are in the wrong place, they are with the wrong people. Think about how this works and why, medically, it makes sense. A person who has an undefined G (Identity, Self) Center is vulnerable to taking in more toxins and other things from outside than a person who has a defined G (Identity, Self) Center. Thus, it is very easy for people with an undefined G Center (Identity, Self) to end up around forces and in situations that are detrimental to them. [There is no evidence for what Ra says on a physical health level. However, Ra's statement about a person with an undefined G Center (Self) picking up the energy around them is valid, and how they handle it is unique to them and their consciousness.]

It is very important for people with an undefined G Center (Self) to know their Type and to understand the nature of the undefined G Center (Self). People with an undefined G Center (Self), who are not living out their Type, are always feeling lost; they are looking for love for their own sense of themselves, and they are trying to hold onto it when they have an experience they value. The moment these people are not living out their Type, and they do not understand how the undefined G Center (Self) works, that is when deterioration in the liver begins. [People with an undefined G Center (Self) do not feel as Ra described them. Do your own research. Ra's psychological interpretations of what people with undefined or defined Centers are not based on clinical data. As a clinician, how someone feels based on their active or undefined Centers is more based on the total picture than on any given Center. Do not assume there are negative feelings in someone who has an undefined G Center.]

As a medical professional, any time you see someone who is jaundiced, you are dealing with someone who is having an identity crisis. [You cannot assume that jaundice is related to an identity crisis. It may be related to infection, alcohol excess, hemolytic anemia, and anatomical defects, among other causes.] That is the root of it. People with undefined G Center (Self) can be very healthy as long as they accept that they have to be initiated into things in life and that they do not have to make a bond with the initiator.

People with an undefined G Center (Self) are very privileged in life because other people are always ready to initiate them. But at the same time, if they are not following their Type, they can be initiated into all kinds of things that are very unhealthy for them. The Manifestor with the undefined G Center (Self) can spontaneously jump into things that are very unhealthy for them.

People with a defined G (Identity, Self) Center, however, have a sense of who they are, and they can know who they are and what they need. They must be living their Type (cf. Primer #1 Types [page 7 in this book]) in order to be true to who they are.

If you have an undefined G (Identity, Self) Center and you enter a place that does not feel right for you, or you do not feel good where you are, leave. See if you feel different.

Do not allow yourself to be initiated into experiences of any kind that are not right for you. Do not, by the same token, initiate a child with an undefined G (Identity, Self) Center into something that is not right for them. If you have a child with an undefined G (Identity, Self) Center, if that child does not like being somewhere or with someone, do not encourage and force the child to learn to "like it." Let the child find a comfort zone that does feel good. Change the environment so the initiation becomes a happy and healthy one.

> The Self Center is an important Center for many reasons. It is likely that the Self Center also relates to the lungs and to the circulation of oxygenated blood from the heart to the rest of the body. In working with the Body Map, be cognizant that there is not a one-to-one correspondence between the Body Map and human physiology. Ra made many assumptions that did not hold up medically or scientifically, either statistically or clinically. Use clinical judgment when talking to clients and be wary of saying anything to them that could undermine their confidence in themselves or the integrity of their health.
>
> In my Human Design Mental/Waking World Chart, I am a Manifestor with an undefined G Center (Self). If I consider only the Human Design Mental/Waking World Chart and not my Integrated Noble Energy Maps®, I would be seen as someone who needs to be initiated by someone. I have always been a self-directed person who has followed my own inner knowing and avoided any unhealthy practices strongly. In my Integrated Noble Energy Maps®, I am a strong Manifesting Generator with a strong G Center (Self). Most people in their Integrated Noble Energy Maps® have a G Center. In psychology, generalized statements miss the nuances of individual differences, the unique nature of our DNA, and its expression in our

manifesting life. Ra taught these classes before much of the newer science was released.

The Heart Center / The Ego Center

Along with the Solar Plexus Center, the Heart Center (Figure 13) is a primary place for disease. The Heart Center is where people get really sick. The Heart Center is where almost all pressure is on the mundane plane. [Ra's statements about the Heart Center and illness did not hold up scientifically on 5,000 cases. The term Ego Center is misleading. In the field of psychology, the Ego refers to the conscious mind as distinct from the Id, the unconscious mind, and the Superego, the higher mind or values a person holds. These are Freudian terms that are general and have become misused in common parlance. In vernacular language, the Ego refers to how someone presents oneself and often has a negative connotation with the term, "Ego," meaning that someone is "full of themselves." In my view, the Heart Center does not deserve that negative connotation.]

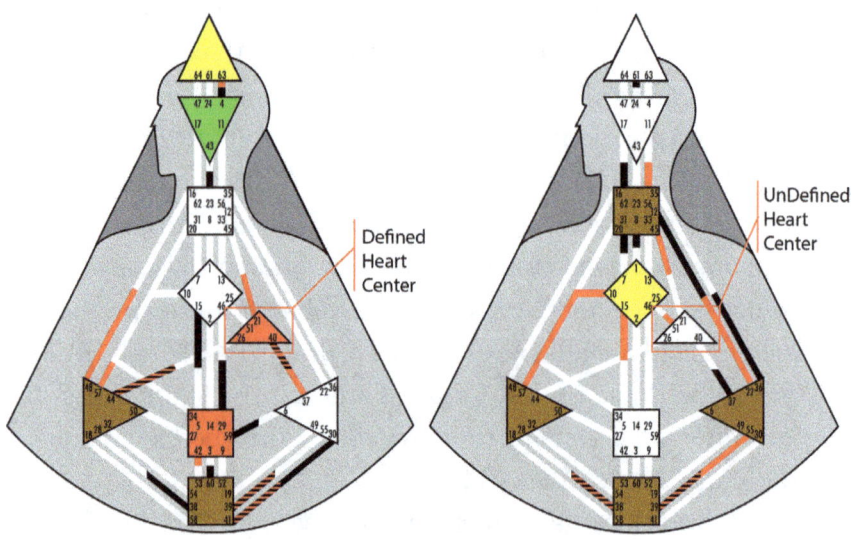

Figure 13: The Heart Center

Pressure, on the day-to-day level, comes out of the Heart Center because we have both the will and the capacity to be able to survive materially. All of us are driven by that. The whole Ego Circuit, of which the Heart Center is a part, is routed through the Heart Center, so everything about the tribe, everything about the community, and everything about the material plane is all there. All of us have been conditioned from our birth to think that there is free will, that it is up to us, and that we have the power; we have all heard, "Go get it!" [Ra believed that Humans have "no choice," contrary to psychological evidence to the contrary. At three months of age, a baby exercises volition and choice in how to relate to their environment. A strong developmental marker that psychologists and pediatricians look at in a normal baby's development is when they reach for objects and exercise their freedom of choice.]

> My factor analyses of Human Design circuitry, as described by Ra, did not show any pattern of reliability or validity in this concept.

The Heart Center is enormously complex at a biological level. The 21st Gate is the heart muscle itself. The 40th Gate is the stomach. The 26th Gate is the thymus gland, where the T-cells are made. The B-cells are made in the 44th Gate. [B-cells are made continuously in the bone marrow. T-cells precursors leave the bone marrow for the thymus. Lymph nodes channels and vessels are located throughout the body.] In the 51st Gate is the gall system, the gall bladder. There is significant biology associated with the Heart Center: heart, stomach, gall bladder, and immune protection. All of these major organs of the body have a Gate associated with them in the Heart Center. It becomes clear immediately that the Heart Center is a source of many physical problems. [Statistical data on 30,000 cases did not validate this statement by Ra. There was no statistical significance in people who died of heart attacks compared to people who did not die of heart attacks based on a defined or open Heart Center.] Look at our common health problems; almost all of them can be linked to the Heart Center. The Heart Center connects all the major organs of the body. For example, the gall bladder and the liver meet (Gate 51 and Gate 25) in the channel connecting the G-Center to the Heart Center. [The Heart Center is a key Center related to health. Just how it relates is yet to be determined and delineated.] Dealing with the Heart Center is essential. It is one of the easiest ways to prevent many illnesses, particularly heart disease.

It is very common to see Manifestors and Generators with heart disease - they are natural energy Types. They recognize, inherently, within their own mechanism that they can "do" and they can "act." The people in their lives want to saddle their energy. The way they do that is by getting them to make promises, which is the most dangerous thing for a person with an undefined Heart Center to do. People tell them, "You promised to love me, you promised to work for me, you promised to do this," etc. They saddle them to that energy, and then the individual with the undefined Heart Center slowly begins to deteriorate. It is never healthy for an individual with an undefined Heart Center (Ego) to put themselves in a situation where they have to be willful. [Again, my statistics on 5,000 Heart Attack patients did not validate Ra's statements.]

Anyone with an undefined Heart Center is really in danger. They are always going to be prospective patients. Normally, in the life process, people with an undefined Heart Center are almost exclusively the window of illness. People with an undefined Heart Center are always going to be vulnerable, and they are going to be vulnerable in places that are really dangerous to their health. [This is an unsubstantiated statement and, if repeated to someone with an open Heart Center, may, in fact, be damaging to them. It is not true.]

A Manifestor with an undefined Heart Center is someone with a potential heart attack who is walking around just waiting to die. If a person with an undefined Heart Center does not make a promise, there is nothing wrong with their heart. It is as simple as that. It is never healthy for an individual with an undefined Heart Center to put themselves in a situation where they have to be willful. [This statement could be for everyone.]

It is important to tell people with an undefined Heart Center that the most dangerous thing in the world for them is to make promises. No promises. A person can respond according to their Type, e.g., someone can invite a person with an undefined Heart Center to meet them tomorrow, and they can respond, "Yes, that is correct." But they cannot say, "I promise that I will see you tomorrow." People who have an undefined Heart Center should never say, "I will." [Most individuals need time to reconsider what is right for them and should avoid promises. Timing is most important in commitments.]

Most people with an undefined Heart Center assume that everybody has free will and that everybody can be willful. They assume that making a promise is special. To honor a promise and all of these things is very special. But that is about people with a defined Heart Center. Someone with a defined Heart Center has to make a promise; if they do not, nobody trusts them. People with a defined Heart Center have to say, "I will do this." Someone with an undefined Heart Center starts dying if they say, "I will do this." [These statements do not hold up clinically or statistically and can do harm.]

A person with a defined Heart Center who is not willful can also end up sick. For instance, a person who has Gate 21 with a defined Heart Center needs to be in control. If they are not in control, they are breaking their inner promise to their nature themselves. They destroy that very capacity within themselves. A person with activation in Gate 21 needs to determine where they live, what they eat, and what they wear. This is crucial for them. If they do not have control, they can end up with a disturbed stomach, and often, for them, it is the acid in the stomach that causes the problem. The chemistry of their stomach does not work properly. [Check this out for yourself, and do not assume it is true for your clients.]

America has a food problem. The stomach is critical in all of this. The Heart Center is all about diet. Again, it works in many different ways. Depending on the Type, a person can truly find out what diet is healthy for them so their stomach can work properly.

A person with an undefined Splenic Center (immune system) along with an undefined Heart Center will find homeopathy and vegetarianism healthy for them. Someone who has a defined Splenic Center that connects to the Throat Center does not benefit from homeopathy. A person with a defined Splenic Center connected to the stomach, the Heart Center, can eat like a bear and can eat anything. [None of these statements are valid. What Ra said about illness and its associated Gates and Lines also did not hold up scientifically. We need more data and more research in this area.]

Someone with an undefined Heart Center automatically has problems with their stomach. [Not true.] However, the problems that develop will depend on who is in their life. For example, a person with an undefined Heart Center whose partner defines that Center may end up eating things with their partner that really are not good for them, simply because the partner is defining their Heart Center. When their partner goes away on a trip, and the person makes a meal that they would normally have with their partner, they spend the whole night suffering because they are eating something that is not good for them. This information is important diagnostically. [Ask, don't tell. Collect data. Be discerning.]

People with an undefined Heart Center need to look after their stomachs. They have to be careful about what they put in. They can easily suffer from indigestion and stomach pain.

A person who is not living out their Type, who is not living out what is there, whether it is defined or undefined, can end up with a lot of difficulties. The stomach is very sensitive at this level and is, thus, extremely vulnerable.

Gallstones are also very common in people with an undefined Heart Center. Particularly in women, problems with the gall bladder are often the first indication of heart disease. [Ra's statement in 2000 was insightful. It is now known that there is an association between gallbladder issues and heart disease. However, heart issues are also multifactorial and may be related to genetics, stress, inflammation, hypertension, and smoking. Its relationship to cholesterol is being questioned by many.] **Problems show up in the gall bladder first because the gall bladder is an initiating channel. So, when someone has gallbladder problems or stones, as a professional, you know right away that if they continue being willful or if they continue trying to live improperly out of their undefined Heart Center, they will end up with heart disease.** [We have no substantiation of this hypothesis. Based on the data we do have, it is likely that these hypotheses of Ra's will not hold up to statistical analysis. Medical issues are much more multifactorial than an open or defined Center.]

Control has a bad name in this society. Living your Design and honoring the Design of those around you puts things like control in perspective.

After all, it is not a bad thing for someone who has the 21st Gate to need or want control over their own home, food, and clothes; it is natural. It is not bad for someone with no activation of the 21st Gate to let someone else carry the responsibility of choosing their home, their food, and their clothes; the specifics of these items do not matter to them as they do to the person with the activated 21st Gate. It is similar in other areas and other Centers and activations. "Design" carries no judgment any more than blue eyes are better or worse than brown eyes. The person has what they were dealt with, and to be who you are, the best you can be for your potential is what you are here to live.

> Because the Heart Center is directly connected through Channel 21-45 to the Heart Muscle itself, it is essential to consider breath and breathing as a therapeutic practice for anyone with this Channel defined. I often suggest to clients who have this Channel activated that they pay attention to

> their breathing, note when they are stressed and when they are relaxed, and note differences in their breathing. Empowering your clients to test suggestions to determine if they fit personally is always best.

Someone with an undefined Heart Center (Ego) does not know how to value themselves. They often sell themselves short. It is especially important for someone who has an undefined Heart Center (Ego) to work for themselves and learn to value themselves or at least know that they tend to undervalue themselves.

The Sacral Center

The Sacral Center is an incredibly powerful motor. The Sacral Center is second in complexity to the Throat Center, with nine Gates. Many aspects of other centers reside in the Sacral Center. It is an energy vortex operating in a spiral in the body. The Sacral Center relates to the life force energy itself, which operates as a generator, and once turned on, it never turns off. People with the Sacral Center defined, turned on, thus, have enormous power that can work for them generatively or that can become "degenerative."

When people are living out their Type, when they are waiting and responding, they can become healthy quickly. As a Generator, someone with a defined Sacral Center, you must wait to respond to others, never to initiate. This is crucial for you to understand. People in your life must ask you if something is "right" for you.

It is important for the person with a defined Sacral Center to recognize that they are not here to initiate things, even if they are a Manifesting Generator. They are here to respond, nothing else. And the response comes through waiting. Understand that responding is very versatile. You can respond as a Generator to many things: to people, to questions, to the environment. But you cannot initiate things for others or yourself. Your power is not determined in that way. The moment an individual with a defined Sacral Center tries to manifest that is the moment when the Sacral Center becomes degenerative and can lead to all kinds of problems. [It is important to look at the Four Worlds, especially in the design of a Generator, to see where and when Channels turn on and off. Many Generators, when they know what is right and aligned for them, are capable of taking the right action for themselves, especially if they are, in fact, a Manifesting Generator in their Integrated Noble Energy Maps®.]

A Generator who does not live out what it is to be a Generator, that is, they wait to respond, shortens their life. [We have no data supporting this statement.] The Sacral Center (Figure 14) can easily move from being a generating field to being a degenerating field. It is very easy for the Sacral Center to become very degenerative.

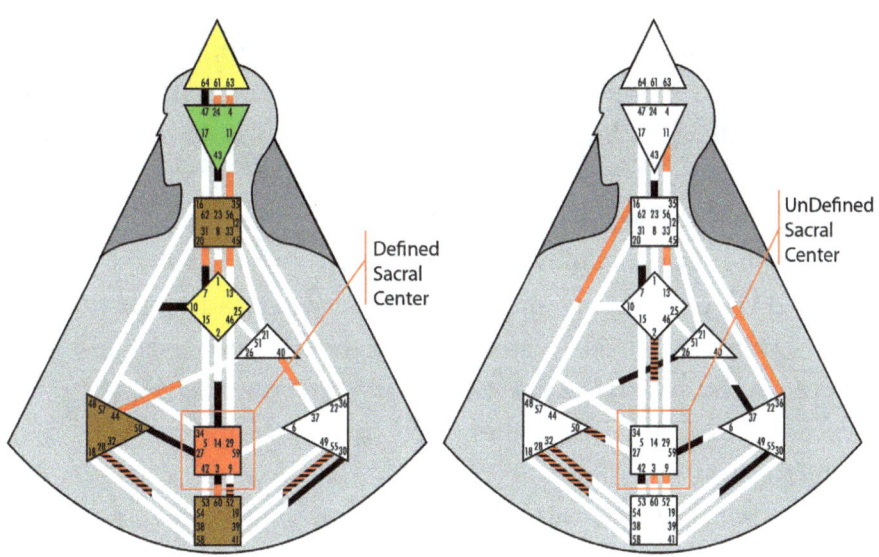

Figure 14: The Sacral Center

Most degenerative Sacral Center problems are related to physical depression in the body, which comes in through the form of energy. People with degenerative Sacral Centers are chronically depressed; they are people who are locked into things, and they cannot get out. The typical thing is for Generators to get stuck. They get stuck in disease. They get stuck in therapies. They get stuck in rehabilitation. They just get stuck. [We have no evidence of specific diseases associated with how a Generator responds or does not respond. And we have no evidence of a Generator being "stuck." Generally, my clients who are Generators know what is right for them, and when honored for their inner guidance, they feel healthy and empowered. All Types, when not acknowledged at their core level of being, feel dissonance and attempt to re-align.] The simple awareness of the need for a Generator to respond to questions rather than initiate can allow them the opportunity for metamorphosis, which, once begun, allows them to get unstuck and become who they are.

If a person with a defined Sacral Center says, "I want that person for my lover," they will end up with some sort of health problem if they get that lover. It can be a minor problem, such as a yeast infection. As soon as the Sacral Center is not operating properly, the person with the Sacral Center definition is in danger. [This hypothesis is unsupported.]

People with the 27th Gate may be susceptible to mononucleosis, aids, and herpes, all of which come in through the 27-50 Channel. [Based on the analysis of AIDS patients who had the 27th Gate, there was no statistical significance in their incidence of aids compared to those with the 27th Gate who did not have AIDS. All of Ra's medical hypotheses regarding specific diseases did not hold up to statistical scrutiny.]

The Sacral Center does not speak in words like the Throat Center can. It has no verbal language of words. Instead, it has the language of sounds: primal life force sounds. The sound of grunts and groans and growls.

A person who has a defined Sacral Center responds with "uh-huh" ("yes") or "un-un" ("no"). These sounds are key for the Generator to know if their response comes from their true power and Authority of the Self.

As you become aware of the Sacrally defined person, notice who in your life uses "uh-huh" and "un-un" as a response frequently. Notice if you use those sounds. When someone eats, do they make those kinds of primal sounds? When someone hugs you, or when you hug someone else, does either person or both make those sounds? It is an awareness of great importance when you begin to notice how to ask a Generator for their true response and when they begin to live from that response. Their whole life can change.

Because a Generator is a natural power source, when they wait, everyone wants their power. People come to them, and they do not meet the kind of resistance that they are vulnerable to meeting when they are living out their not self. A Generator who waits to respond will find that things begin to work more easily in their life because the resistance they have met previously begins to fall away. When Generators are first told to wait to respond, they are often fearful that they will not be asked and that nothing will happen to them in their life. This fear comes out of not understanding the nature of auras and how they mechanically interact.

What happens when Generators try the experiment of waiting is that they see that because they are actually an energy type, others want their energy. They are a powerful energy source, and when they do not initiate, others do, and the others come to them to tap into their energy of response. It is a very reassuring experience for Generators when they begin to live the experiment of who they really are. When they enter into things out of their true response, they enter into things correctly, and things work for them.

Generators are vulnerable to frustration because they are hard workers who can get stuck with things that are not right for them. When Generators live in a way that does not come out of their true Sacral nature, they may find that they are prone to diseases that find their way to one of their undefined centers and manifest there. However, Generators who live out of their true response are here to be healthy.

Gate 27 is the Gate of our genetic strategy in caring. So, the moment that the Sacral Center is not operating properly, it turns into a complete lack of care with no protection for the immune system.

The person with an undefined Sacral Center is interested in life and how it works. That is what generating is all about. It also means that someone with an undefined Sacral Center is deeply conditioned by the outside sacral field. People with an undefined Sacral Center can bring all kinds of things into their undefined Sacral field. What this dynamic does, most often, is to cause people who are otherwise healthy to enter into relationships and to become ill. [Consider how an open Sacral Center might function in a person who is in touch with their inner responses. Awareness of your inner responses is key to health. This fact is true for everyone regardless of whether their Sacral Center is defined or not.]

For example, if one person is logical and the other is not logical, both of them end up with a format energy that does not belong to them. They are taking into their bodies a format energy with which they do not naturally deal. This dynamic in couples can create illness in each of them.

Women who have an undefined Sacral Center have the potential for problems with the ovaries. Men who have an undefined Sacral Center have the potential for problems with the testes, and particularly, for problems with their prostate. Undefined Sacral Center people can have serious problems at that level. They tend to have problems with their sexuality simply because it is being conditioned by outside forces.

The most damage is done to people in puberty. Young people with an undefined Sacral Center do not understand how their sexuality works. This point is particularly important for young people because they can suffer a great deal of damage from being initiated into sexuality in ways that are improper for them. [While this is a valid statement, it does not have to do with a defined or undefined Center.]

Teenagers who have an undefined Sacral Center are vulnerable to being programmed by their first sexual experience and to assume that that experience defines the way sex is. [No evidence exists to verify this statement.] They have no way within themselves to know what their true sexuality is like because they have an undefined Sacral Center. It is, thus, very important for children to be taught who they are early and for their sacral energy definition to be recognized as defined or as undefined so they can be taught about themselves and who they are. [Ra is making significant assumptions about the lack of awareness and consciousness of people. In my 50 plus years of clinical experience as a sex therapist, I have not found Ra's statements about sexuality to be accurate or valid. If you are coaching or doing readings for clients, please listen to them before you make assumptions about how they experience their Sacral energy. Look at their designs and, at the most, suggest that they revisit past experiences and consider how aligned those experiences were with their deepest Self. Move their conscious awareness to their inner process so they can assess their balance for themselves.]

Individuals with an undefined sacral Center may not have normal sexual activity. The person with an undefined Sacral Center can be totally turned off. The person can be asexual. A person with an undefined Sacral Center can have no sexual response whatsoever and, at the same time, can become instantly sexual because of conditioning. Considering how important sexuality is for human beings and the force of sexuality when you are reaching puberty, many problems that arise out of the Sacral Center are just conditioned problems. Conditioning leads to all kinds of problems later in life, e.g., "I do not want to have sex because sex is like that." Many people with undefined Sacral Centers have had their first sexual experience distort their sexuality for the rest of their lives.

> Throughout his work, Ra refers to conditioning. As I stated before, conditioning has many variants in the psychological field, and most individuals I have worked with resist the kind of conditioning that Ra is talking about. Throughout my fifty

years of clinical practice, all of my clients know who they are and seek recognition for their creative intelligence and inner sense of themselves. When someone has an open Sacral Center, they do well when asked about their inner responses, but they know what belongs to them in their open energy field versus what does not feel aligned internally. This discernment is key to focus on with someone with an undefined Sacral Center. As professionals, we aim to help our clients open to their "inner knower" and innate wisdom about who they are. The Human Design and Noble Energy Maps® are tools that guide them in ways that empower their consciousness.

A very important point to note is that because the Sacral Center is a generative system with the ability to keep life going, it needs conditioning in the person with an undefined Sacral Center. People with an undefined Sacral Center always need to have their spirits lifted. It is very important for undefined Sacral Center individuals to have their spirits lifted when they are ill. Otherwise, they can very easily get into a degenerative state. [A person with an undefined Sacral Center can use meditation to feel their inner energy core. Because of transits and the Sacral definition of transits, everyone has had the experience of being a Generator by the time they are three months old. By the time we are three months old, all the cosmic energies in the 360-degree wheel have imprinted us energetically. Thus, we all have the memories to call upon in terms of knowing how we function and who we feel most comfortable being.]

Sexually related infections are the most common problem for the undefined Sacral Center individual. You are going to find infertility in the undefined Sacral Center being. Everyone with an undefined Sacral Center is not infertile. Still, the Sacral Center, when undefined, does not operate consistently or properly, and these people can end up having difficulties with fertility. [We have no evidence for this statement as fact.]

In many cases of women who have had readings, who have said

they cannot have a child, and who have an undefined Sacral Center, the problem has usually turned out to be with their partner. The problem has to do with the way the couple connects in the Sacral Center. When dealing with an undefined Sacral Center person, you are often dealing with a touchy subject with clients because you are going to the bone of their existing relationships. Awareness can have a detrimental impact on their relationship. Whether that impact is positive or negative is another story. The subject is certainly something that affects individuals right away. [When comparing couples, be very cautious about drawing any conclusions such as the ones Ra has drawn. Relationships have many layers, and any combination of patterns can work in a couple if they are conscious and open to working together to align energetically.]

The most important time for an undefined Sacral Center person is from 0-18 years. That is when the real damage can be done. It is not the same kind of problem later in life. [Remember that when you consider how an individual is designed as an integrated being living in Four Worlds, it is likely that most individuals know and hold on to their identity at the core, despite resistance and input from outside themselves. It is a testament to human nature that individuals suffer rather than abdicate their self-awareness.]

If you have before you a person with a defined Sacral Center, you automatically have a Generator. Generators are only going to be healthy when they are acting out of their response. They need to appreciate what it means not to meet resistance in their life. If you are a Generator, make sure that you have a healthcare practitioner who asks you what is right for you. Make sure your doctor says, "Do you want this medicine?" "Do you want this vitamin?" "Do you want to do this?" It is critical for you. Also, make sure that the other people in your life ask you what is right for you and that that sacral response is respected and honored by you and by them. [Making sure what you do and are ingesting is right for you holds true for all Types, not just Generators.] When a Generator waits to be asked, they get their "terms" and face no resistance. Their whole health and well-being depend on waiting for a response. Everything works when a Generator is asked to use its power. Nothing works when they push their power out when they initiate. Although I was identified in the Human Design Mental/Waking World Chart as a Manifestor, I did not act like a Manifestor. Instead, I waited to know what I knew when I knew it, and when it was right for me internally and in terms of timing, I would take action. This pattern in myself confirms to me that a Generator can manifest when the timing is right to do so. Remember, astrological transits make everyone, regardless of Human Design Type, a Manifesting Generator at some time during every month.

A Generator is a natural power source and can wait because everyone wants their power. If a Generator waits, people will come to it, and then it will not meet resistance. Usually, a Generator's biggest gripe is that no one is going to ask them. The moment you tell a Generator that they have to wait and that they have to be asked, the first thing that happens to them is that they find that concept incredibly frustrating.

Generators are an energy Type. As an energy person, they have been conditioned all their life to do. Everybody tells them how much energy they have, and everybody is really impressed with the fact that they can work and work and work. Typical pain for Generators is being locked into doing things that they loathe. When Generators are told that they have to wait, they are terrified that nobody will ask for their response because they do not understand what an aura is. They do not understand that whenever they come into someone else's aura, the other can feel all their power. Their Sacral Center pulls others to ask them. It is a physical, mechanical process. [This hypothesis about how the Sacral Center functions has not been substantiated clinically or statistically.]

The Generator always has the opportunity to be instantly healthy, instantly transformed, and instantly enlightened. All of these things are possible. It is simply a matter of being totally surrendered to waiting and to being asked.

In the medical sense, when you deal with someone who has a defined Sacral Center, you are dealing with someone who is going to have a slow-burning sickness in their life unless they are living out their nature. In other words, slowly but surely, the frustration Generators experience is just going to dig into them, and it will find its place. It will find its place in one of the undefined Centers, and it will eventually come to the surface as a disease or as a problem. [This hypothesis is unsubstantiated.]

Generators are really here to be very healthy. All of our societies and civilizations have been built on the backs of Generators. Nobody works harder than a Generator. Of course, the vast majority of Generators work at things that are not right for them. There is an enormous amount of frustration out there. [We need to test this statistically. I have not found this to be true clinically.]

The key to healing a Generator is to understand that they get stuck at different levels of healing. This point is very important. The gears get stuck. It is always like that for them. Generators need to enter into things correctly; otherwise, they cannot stay with it. Doctor's offices are filled with all kinds of Generator patients who come in, start a procedure, and quit. They just walk away. They get frustrated with the treatment because they do not see the improvement. Improvement cannot occur unless a Generator enters into it properly. In almost all cases, Generators are just told to "do this" treatment." Remember that the Generator has to be asked in order to be helped. As a professional, you have to be attentive to their Design in order for them to be helped. [Many Generators are intuitively in touch with what resonates with them and what does not. From a clinical perspective, any good clinician would ask their client about what feels aligned or not and would never push treatment that is not healing and comfortable for their client.]

The future of healing lies in regular visitation and contact. In other words, the practitioner will have an ongoing relationship so they can see the differences in their patients.

The Sacral Center is not aware. It is a diaphragm; it will speak for whatever connects to it. [The Sacral Center is not medically categorized as a diaphragm.] Most people who are Generators do not understand, and they think their Sacral Center is their authority. They think that the Sacral Center has some kind of neural activity, that it is working all this out, and that it is making decisions. The Sacral Center makes no decisions at all. What is connected to the sacral guides it.

Some of the most aware people on the planet are people with their Splenic Center connected to the Sacral Center. The Splenic Center is the only real awareness we have. The Mind cannot run a life, and yet it is crazy-making while it is not running a life. The Mind is an interesting thing to share, but it is not something inside that ever has any authority.

The Splenic Center (immune system) is the only true awareness Center that we have. In someone who has the Sacral Center connected to the Splenic Center, every time you ask them a question, they are really answering with whether what you are asking them is healthy for them or not. It can be very confusing if they try to put it into mental terms. The interpretation of the Sacral sound is confusing. They never consciously know the reason for their response about what is healthy for them. The mind, which rules the way our mental awareness works, has no relationship to our lymphatic system. The Spleen-Sacral connection is all about the lymph system.

The Generator has to trust what is there in their response; they must learn not to ask, "Why?" but just to accept the response and see what comes of it.

The Splenic Center

The Splenic Center (Immune System) (Figure 15) is an awareness Center. Of the three awareness Centers, the Splenic Center (Immune System) is the weakest because it has the capacity to respond only in the moment, in the Now. It can only quietly inform its host about its awareness in the Now, and thus, it can easily be ignored by the host and thus damaged.

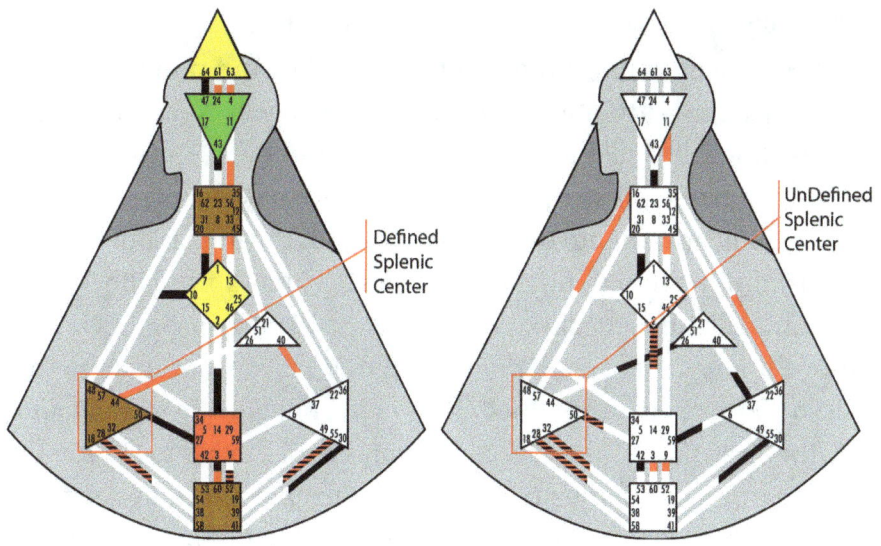

Figure 15: The Splenic Center

All awareness Centers are rooted in fear. In the Splenic Center (immune system) (Figure 15), there are survival fears. In the Ajna Center, there are anxiety fears, i.e., the mental anxiety of not being able to communicate. In the Solar Plexus Center (emotional system), there is nervousness. [Although these statements are not verified statistically, they do hold up from a common-sense perspective.]

The Splenic Center (Immune System) is the Center of the body that controls the lymphatic System. The Splenic Center is incredibly weak, not in its capacity to function properly, but in its capacity to inform its host of what to do to function properly. A person with a defined Splenic Center (immune system) with Splenic authority must honor their gut feeling when they get one. If they do not honor their gut feeling in that moment, they never have the opportunity again and they have to pay the price of ignoring what their gut feeling told them. [The Splenic Center activates intuition and inner knowing. When Ra describes a "gut" feeling in the Splenic Center, he is referring to knowing intuitively and instinctively but with a quality that differentiates Splenic knowing from Sacral knowing. Clinically, this perspective holds up to scrutiny.]

People can damage their Splenic Center (immune system) by not paying any attention to it. Those people who keep on saying, "I just knew it, I just knew it," say, "I just knew it," until they are dead. If a person is not paying attention to that message, they are really going to run into difficulties. Without the information about their immune functioning this person is vulnerable to illness and to damaging their health. [Illness and its etiology are not verified based on defined or undefined Centers. In fact, what Ra hypothesized about open and defined Centers did not hold up statistically.]

The first thing that you, as a professional, have to do for the defined Splenic Center (immune system) person is to get them to be able to accept what it means to be truly a spontaneous person, given that for that person, there is no emotional authority. They must truly recognize how important it is to truly be a spontaneous person. The mind does not understand the Splenic Center (immune system). The mind just does not understand the spleen and the mind cannot communicate with it. The Ajna (mind) and the Splenic Center (immune system) do not speak the same language.

It is an incredible irony. The Splenic Center, the immune system, has been there forever, in a sense. Humans have always had a spontaneous response to survival because life is all about survival. Life is not about the spirit, which is really the emotional business. Life is really just about the basics of survival. That is the beauty of the Splenic Center (immune system). When a person pays attention to it, they really get the reward. The immune system reacts. The reaction is immediate in the way it operates the biology. The immune system does not know how to continually struggle because it is inherently weak to begin with. A person must pay attention to the Splenic Center (immune system) when it tells them something or they are really in a lot of trouble.

The mind is always telling people what they should do. The mind is always very busy. The mind is always trying to take control, and it is always trying to have a coup d'état. The mind really wants to be the boss desperately. The mind has all the concerns about strategy and plot, thinking that is what being healthy is all about. But it is not. Being healthy is about just allowing a defined Splenic Center (immune system) person to wait to see the truth at any given moment. Then, the person who has Splenic Center (immune system) definition maintains their well-being, their immune system works, and they are healthy. [When Ra talks about the Mind, he does not consider the Creative Intelligence of the Higher Mind that activates through Spiritual/Archetypal and Emotional/Angelic activations. Part of the human journey involves the evolution of consciousness through the lifespan and the refinement of emotional reactions through application of compassion and love.]

People who have powerful immune systems who are Manifestors are really at risk because they do not ask for help. Even when they are ill, and even when things are really there deep inside, they do not necessarily call out for help because there is a part of Manifestors that just assumes that they can make their way through it alone. That is something to pay attention to in the people who are unaware of their design.

When you are looking at a Splenic Manifestor, they need you to encourage them to tell you how they feel and to tell you what is going on and whether they are okay or not. They can end up having Splenic Centers (immune system) that collapse. As a professional, you cannot tell when their immune system is just on the edge of collapsing. The immune system appears no different than then when it is fully strong and healthy. With Manifestors, you have to encourage their trust. Manifestors have to feel like they can ask you without facing resistance. The greatest fear for a Manifestor comes when they are ready to ask for help. They fear then that they will not get what they ask for. Consequently, often, they do not ask for what they need. Their fear is something to be aware of as a professional. Defined Splenic Center (immune system) Manifestors need encouragement to get through their fear of asking for what they need.

> Many of Ra's generalizations about Splenic-defined Manifestors do not track clinically. I have worked with many Splenic Manifestors who are highly intuitive and have great sensitivity to their immune health and its sensitivity. To the degree they honor their inner knowing, they manifest a healthy and strong immune system. Treat each person as unique and read their Body Maps in accord with their energy and their consciousness.

One of the things to see about the symmetry of the Splenic Center (immune system) and the Solar Plexus Center (emotional system) is the relationship between the 50th Gate and the Sixth Gate. The Sixth Gate is where the emotional motor actually is. Whenever you see the Sixth Gate in somebody's design, you know they have work to do. The Sixth Gate is the pH of the body. The Sixth Gate represents the creation of a boundary, like a diaphragm. It is going to be open, or it is going to be closed. It is the openness to intimacy or the openness to reproduction. What we call "closed" is infertility. [Fertility in Gate 6 or Channel 6-59 did not hold up statistically.]

> Gate 59 is a Portal Gate to the Emotional/Angelic World. Ra is right that Gate 6 represents a boundary between the Emotional/Angelic World, the Physical/Biological World, and the Mental/Waking World. My research clinically documents that the Solar Plexus activates emotional energy in the Mental/Waking World and Physical/Biological Worlds only. Through the portal to the Emotional/Angelic World through Gate 59,

> emotional reactivity transforms. Think about the flow of emotional energy and how it impacts you and your clients when there is no Gate 59 to form a transformational Channel for emotional energy.

Within the Sixth Gate, which controls the wave, within the channel of intimacy, are all three patterns that were discussed in the Solar Plexus Center (emotional system) section. The Sixth Gate carries within it the source of all three waves. In the Sixth Gate, the three waves are one.

When you come to the 50th Gate in the Splenic Center in a similar position to the other end of the Sixth Gate, it does the same thing, but it does not create an emotional wave; it creates an awareness frequency. This frequency creates what we call intelligence, what we call consciousness. What we call intelligence or what we call consciousness all come out of the 50th Gate, which is where this awareness originates.

This is why it is called the Gate of Moses, the lawgiver. Gate 50 is the Gate of Values. Out of the 50th Gate flow, the three streams are called instinct, intuition, and taste. Taste is always about right or wrong. In other words, the logical process is always about being able to see right and wrong. The gift there in the logic process is to see right and wrong, but that does not mean that at any moment, the logic is right; it just means the capacity is there. You can see that these three streams are all rooted in one Gate, Gate 50.

Gate 50 deals with how awareness works. The inside channel is the awareness stream of instinct. Gates 54, 32, and 44 are part of this stream. If a person does not have anything in this stream, they are likely to end up with Alzheimer's or memory loss. This stream is where memory is placed in the cell. Cellular memory is here. [No illnesses correlated with defined or undefined Gates or Channels in the study of 30,000 cases. However, I have documented clinically that a person with Gate 50 often awakens with angst. Because Gate 50 is active in the Dream Design and during REM sleep/dreaming crosses neurological pathways between the sleep centers in the brain and the waking cortex, there does seem to be some validity to it activating a person's mission and sense of responsibility as a custodian of their culture and caretaking of others.]

The body has a very complex memory circuit. These Gates are the lowest level of this circuit. This circuit is the base level of memory because this is the memory that is there, that we call instinct, that is at the cellular level. There are higher levels of memory, the 11th Gate or the 56th Gate, for example. People who have the 33rd Gate or the 13th Gate have a very powerful memory. But these are different levels of memory than instinctive memory; these involve identity memory of experience and mental memory. [These Gates are higher frequency Gates in the Tree of Life's Paths of Intelligence. Although Channel 11-56 is in the Ajna Center and connects to the Throat Center, it carries energy of consciousness. Channel 13-33 relates to the Constituting Path of Intelligence in the Tree of Life.]

In the limited research that has been done, the lack of activation in these Gates (there are other factors involved) indicates that something is wrong at the cellular level with the way information is being stored. [This statement is speculative.]

Sounds can heal people who have the individual Gates (38-28) in the Splenic Center (immune system). Individuality is purely acoustic and tonal, and working with music, singing, or simply plain music therapy can help heal these acoustic, tonal people. For many people, having an ongoing soundtrack that had the right kind of musical frequency for them would eliminate the anxiety in their daily lives. The stream of taste deals with the focused process. [Ra's statement has not been validated.]

The most important thing to recognize about the undefined Splenic Center (immune system) is that it is not weak. Recognize that covering it over is dangerous. People with an undefined Splenic Center (immune system) do not necessarily feel good, but that is not bad. However, every time someone with a defined

Splenic Center (immune system) comes to them and makes them feel good, it does not necessarily mean that that is good for them. Often, it can be dangerous. [An undefined Splenic Center makes someone a physical empath, i.e., when around other people, they are sensitive to what the other person feels physically and may "pick their feelings up physically." Marvin is a physical empath and feels in his body what his patients experience. Once Marvin recognized his sensitivity and that he picks up energy this way, he became adept at recognizing what energy belongs to him and what belongs to someone outside of him.]

In many ways, the person with an undefined Splenic Center (immune system) can be the healthiest person on earth. Remember that the white Centers are where wisdom is. The people with an undefined Splenic Center (immune system) are not here to be spontaneous. When they are not being spontaneous, they can actually take things in, in the moment (it is natural for them because it is open). Then, they are able to develop their defense system against what they have taken in so that the next time they meet it, it does not impact them.

These people can become very, very healthy human beings. They need the most lenient healing program possible. A child with an undefined Splenic Center (immune system) gets all the diseases, and the reality is that all you have to do is allow them to heal properly. At the moment that you think they are healthy, you have to give them a few more days. You cannot send them back to school with a runny nose or when there is still a little bit of a cough. No matter what the inconvenience, they need extra time to recover and fully heal. [These statements need to be verified.]

The healing process is crucial. There is no need to be concerned with the immune system itself because it is open. This open Splenic Center (immune system) can be a brilliant immune system because it can learn to adapt and fight anything. Still, it can only learn when it is allowed to fully go through an experience and get to the other side. It has to be completed and finished with it. When the Splenic

Center (immune system) has learned what it needs to learn, this person with the undefined Splenic Center (immune system) can go back into the world. This is true for adults, too.

What often happens, particularly to children, is that the parents do not want them to stay home. Parents have an 8-year-old or a 9-year-old in the house that can drive them crazy, and they have to work two jobs, families, etc. As soon as the child's nose stops running, they send these children back to school, and a week later, the child is very sick again because they have taken in something else. The child's immune system is overloaded, which leads to all kinds of difficulties. [This hypothesis needs verification.]

A person with a defined Splenic Center (immune system) needs regular, allopathic medicine. That person has to deal with modern technology and medicine. As a professional, you already know that, in order to make any impact on a person with a defined Splenic Center (immune system), you are going to have to come in with the big guns. You need something powerful to deal with this defined Splenic Center (immune system).

Because a person with an undefined Splenic Center (immune system) is tremendously sensitive, homeopathic or other energetic medicines will most likely be highly effective as a treatment. Homeopathic medicines are much gentler on people with such sensitive systems and will facilitate helping the system build its strength.

People with a defined Splenic Center (immune system) that is cut off from their Throat Center can be treated with homeopathic remedies. These people need gentle treatment and preventive remedies.

People who live out their Type protect their Splenic Center (immune system). The moment a person lives out their Type, they are not putting stress on their Splenic Center (immune system) and can have and maintain a strong immune system. [All of Ra's hypotheses about medical conditions and treatments are unvalidated. They did not hold up statistically in 30,000 cases or in clinical analysis. However, further study may show validity on a more nuanced level.]

The Solar Plexus Center

The Solar Plexus Center (Emotional System) (Figure 16) is a center that we need to pay a lot of attention to because it is a difficult Center for people to understand and also because it is an area in the body where many disease complexes have their basis. Emotional problems come out in Centers other than the Solar Plexus Center (Emotional System). But when you are looking at someone's Design, whether they have a defined Solar Plexus Center (Emotional System) or not, this Center still represents the same problem in that it represents an area for everyone of great vulnerability.

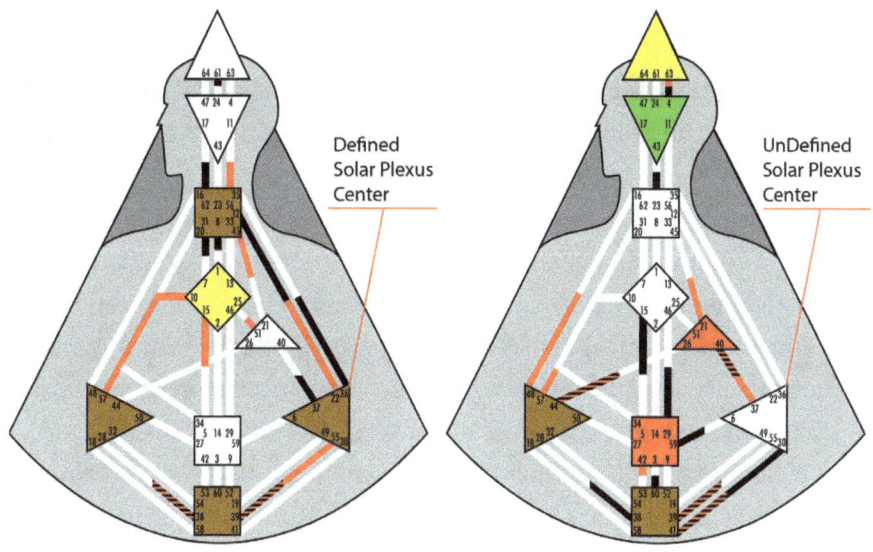

Figure 16: The Solar Plexus

The two areas with the highest frequency of health problems are the Solar Plexus Center (Figure 16) on one side and the Splenic

Center on the other side. One basic about the body graph is its symmetry. The symmetry always needs to be respected.

When you have someone whose Splenic Center (immune system) is defined and whose Solar Plexus (emotional) is undefined, you know the problems are going to be on the Solar Plexus side. The same is true for the other way around. Someone who is defined on the Solar Plexus Center side who has an undefined Splenic Center will have problems on the Splenic Center side. Both of those areas have to do with our well-being, even though the Splenic Center (immune system) is seen as being the primary Center of our immune protection.

It is interesting to note that before 1781, when Herschel discovered Uranus [March 13, 1781], the Splenic Center was a minor Center and was not one of the seven major Centers. With the advent of the industrial age, the growth in population, and the intermingling of cultures, a minor splenic system took on a very powerful value. Evolution then changed us from a seven-energy Center being to a nine-energy Center being. Before 1781, in terms of the original seven Centers, the Solar Plexus Center was the main area for defense in terms of the immune function of people.

> The Kabbalistic Tree of Life shows a ten-centered diagram of a human energy system. In Hindu literature, it is noted that Humans have twelve Chakras. Thus, Ra's interpretation of the change in a human's energy system does not seem congruent with history. The synthesis of the Tree of Life, the Hindu Chakra System, astrology, and the Hexagrams of the I-Ching are the crucial components innovatively combined into the Body Map. Because of the data Ra shared with Marvin and me, it was apparent that the Human Design Body Graph was only one-eighth of a complete system. By adding the Sleep and Dream Designs and the Emotional/Angelic World calculations to the basic Human Design calculations, a scientifically sound integration of the Worlds based on critical developmental

> stages in human development emerged. I call this integrated and scientifically sound system Noble Energy Maps®. It has been validated in more than 15,000 clinical cases.

The energy of the Solar Plexus Center [Emotional/Angelic System] always operates in a wave. It is critical to understand this energy phenomenon because it is key to the strategy of the health of the Solar Plexus Center [Emotional/Angelic System]. The Solar Plexus wave always goes from hope to pain and from joy to despair and back again. The wave occurs over time, not in the now, so it is critical for an individual with the Solar Plexus Center definition to wait for the full cycle of the wave before making any decisions or before assuming any clarity of feeling.

> The wave Ra described is emotional reactivity. It occurs in the Mental/Waking World only because the Solar Plexus Center operates in the Physical/Biological World (25-Gate Matrix) and in the Mental/Waking World (64-Gate Matrix). The Emotional/Angelic World (33-Gate Matrix) has a Portal Gate (Gate 59) that connects to the Solar Plexus through Gate 6. We are energetically designed to be spiritual beings, and emotional reactivity is transformed to its higher frequency vibrations through using our creative intelligence to transform emotional reactivity into higher frequency awareness and understanding. This dynamic interaction between the Worlds was recognized by Ra when we were teaching the Dream Rave (cf. *The Triple Design Matrix* Book) materials and he acknowledged that only when the matrices of the worlds integrated did clarity of functioning become clear.

The defined Solar Plexus Center person is not defined to know in the Now, they are instead designed to wait out their wave of emotional energy and to know through that wave what is right for them. Very often, the person who is emotionally defined finds it difficult to wait out their wave; they have experience after experience in which they make "mistakes" because they make choices without the clarity of time. If they have these experiences repeatedly, eventually, they learn to wait for their emotional wave to pass before they jump into a decision. However, if they have an awareness of their pattern, much pain in their life can be avoided. [Ra is describing emotional Reactivity here. In the Kabbalistic Tree of Life the Solar Plexus and the Splenic Centers must discern truth from emotional reactions and misinformation in order to enter the Paths of Return that activate higher frequencies of consciousness and personal evolution. This balancing of the Splenic and Solar Plexus Centers is described in the twenty-seventh Path of Intelligence on the Tree of Life.]

Another very important aspect to learn about the Solar Plexus Center (Emotional System) is that the power of that energy can make it seem as though the person with the undefined Solar Plexus Center is the person who is emotional. Here is how this dynamic works. The person with an undefined Solar Plexus Center (Emotional System) is open to the energy of the other person. When this undefined Solar Plexus Center person comes into the aura of the person with a defined Solar Plexus Center, this person may act and feel as the Emotionally defined person acts and feels. It is not them. It is not their emotions. Those emotions do not belong to them. [If you have an open Center, you experience all possible energies of that Center, either through transits or through being with someone who has that Center activated. You pick up energy in your open Centers, and your shifting experience of that Center makes you empathic to the energy of that Center.]

Many children are told that they are "too emotional," and they do not understand why that is being said about them because they do not feel emotional. Look at the designs in the family. It is very possible that the parent describing the child as "too emotional" is actually the carrier of the emotional definition and that the child is picking up on that parent's mood and feelings and is reflecting them back as a mirror, only even more extremely than the parent feels the mood. When this kind of dynamic exists and when the child is constantly made to feel responsible for something that is not actually the child, you can begin to see how dysfunction and miscommunication happen.

Often, in working with couples using Design, it becomes apparent that miscommunications arise when one person is defined, and the other one is undefined in the area of the Solar Plexus (Emotional System), and the couple is not aware of who really carries the moods and the energy of emotion. Such miscommunications clear up rapidly by seeing the simple mechanics of Design.

Within a person's Design there are different possible patterns of energy called Formats. The different Formats may affect the way in which a person experiences their emotional energy and is defined by it. [In my research, how an individual experiences their emotional energy depends more the way the Matrices interact and how the multidimensional designs interconnect through the Portal Gates. Timing of how and when connections internally happen makes a difference in how someone perceives energy and manifests it.]

Three Kinds of Emotional Waves

The Abstract Emotional Wave
The abstract emotional wave is the outside stream of energy. The outside stream, the stream of feelings, is all rooted in desire. Desire begins with Gate 41, the only initiating codon we have, and the Gate that begins all experience, desire, and hunger. This is the human experiential way that can never be aware, and it is always rooted in expectation. This initiating codon, the human experiential way, begins with the hunger in Gate 41. Gate 41 is also a Gate of Fantasy. The wave of the abstract stream begins with hunger, desire, or fantasy at a low point seeking experience. It is only when the wave gets to the 30th Gate that it really begins to manifest. It begins to

manifest because the 30th Gate is where the feeling actually takes on its emotional quality. That feeling, that emotional quality then, is something that is going to operate in this wave.

First, there is this low point, and then it goes very quickly to Gate 30, where it plateaus. The wave plateaus, and that plateau can last quite a long time. That plateau lasts until it gets to Gate 36. Gate 36 is the Gate of Crisis, the Gate of Inexperience. It is the Gate most capable of penetrating the surface. That is why Gate 36 is all about intercourse at the sexual level. Gate 36 is simply about needing to penetrate, not for the value of it, not for the quality of it, just solely for the experience. Gate 36 is about having the experience and going through it.

From Gate 41 to Gate 30 to Gate 36, the wave has gone up, kind of a slanted wave; it then goes along on the plateau, and Gate 36 is just waiting to get to Gate 35. When it gets to Gate 35, it crashes like a stone. Over. This is the way abstract people go through their waves.

There is a slow climb up from the fantasy, the dream, to the feeling, which gets inside of them and starts burning, starting the plateau. Then they get to Gate 36, where there is this need and the readiness for penetration. The moment the penetration takes place, the moment the 36th Gate meets the 35th Gate, at that moment the experience is over; there is the crash. [There is no substantiation of this hypothesis. Statistical analysis of Circuits as Ra defined them did not hold up in Multivariant Analysis of Variance nor in Factor Analyses, including Rotational Factor Analyses on 30,000 cases.]

When you are dealing with someone with a defined Solar Plexus Center (emotional system), and they have aspects of definition in that stream, the first thing you know is the way their wave is working. The crisis for them is this falling off the edge. That is why the voice of the 35th Gate can say: "I have been there and done that." In other words, "I know what that experience is like. I do not need to climb that thing again only to have this crash because now I know what that is all about."

The most dangerous thing for people with a defined Solar Plexus

Center, i.e., experiential people, is to repeat things. They need new experiences. Then, they can accept the drop. What most people who operate emotionally out of experience do not realize is that everything for them is really impersonal. This is where they get into trouble. This is not about the person; for example, in their sexuality, it is impersonal. It is about the experience itself. Once they recognize that, it is very healthy. [We need to collect data to verify this statement.]

What happens to them emotionally is that they are the ones that we really call crisis people. We see this incredible drop and they experience this incredible drop. They are the ones who really fall into crisis, and, as professionals, you have to be able to care for them right away. In other words, when they go down, they really go down, and it is quite a crash for them. At the psychic level, at the emotional level, that can be extremely painful. They go through the high of the experience, they go along on that plateau, and then, all of a sudden, it is over, and they crash, and they feel devastated. This wave is not aware.

That is why abstract emotional people have to be so careful about the nature of the experiences they enter into. What the experience is does not matter as long as they have achieved clarity from waiting out their wave before entering into it. The experience itself does not matter as long as they have given it emotional authority and entered into it properly. Highs and lows are part of the wave. Knowing this pattern and knowing that it is chemistry without any particular meaning attached to this wave pattern can help them avoid great despair. Then they are living their nature and can be healthy. [Ra was describing emotional reactivity and was right that someone feeling emotional needs to consider how to transform their reactivity into a higher frequency that advances their consciousness and awareness.]

The person who has the Solar Plexus Center defined through the abstract wave is very different than the person who has the Solar Plexus Center undefined. The person who has the Solar Plexus

Center undefined lives it out as an extreme condition by the other. In other words, somebody can pull them down. They are vulnerable to being pulled down. They step into another's aura, they experience the aura, and they are pulled into it when, in fact, it does not belong to them. This awareness is important for them to know what Self is and what is "Not Self." [A person with open Centers functions as an empath.] This process is always more powerful when in an undefined Solar Plexus Center (emotional system).

In terms of illness, people in this wave plateau do not always know they are ill. Illness seems to come very suddenly, and it comes after an experience. However, the illness can be sitting there, under the surface. They have an experience, do something, and it looks like the illness came on suddenly, but it actually had been there, under the surface, on the plateau, for quite a while. [Diagnostic or medical data is not available, but statistical research did not find correlations between definitions and illness.]

The Individual Emotional Wave

The Center stream is about individuality and passion. Individuality connected through the Solar Plexus Center (emotional system) by this channel of individuality (39-55-22-12) tells you, as a professional, that this person is melancholic. You know this very important fact about this individual automatically if they have these connections. When melancholy is not understood, the resulting depression makes it practically impossible to heal them. Melancholy is a chemistry and should never have a reason put on it. Women understand this chemistry, as it is similar to their menstrual cycle. Chemistry is not a reason. When this concept is grasped, people can see that melancholy is creatively productive. [According to Ra, the individual format is from the Root Center to the Sacral Center through Channel 60-3. This may operate in a pulse-like fashion and provide the individual with this format a sense of start-and-stop energy. Procrastination or doubt can creep into their energy if they are unclear about their intentions. However, we have no data on the format energies and need validation to determine their function and impact. The circuitry hypothesized by Ra did not hold up statistically, although it makes sense logically.]

Remember that the Individual wave operates in a pulse and thus has a breath between pulses. It may have a long plateau that is either high or low. But it is chemistry, nothing more. The individual emotional wave is an extremely long plateau, but it is nothing other than a plateau. It can be very deceiving. The plateau can be low or high, but it is just a plateau. Eventually, whether it is every ten minutes or every ten years, it spikes. When it spikes, it goes up immediately or, instantly, it goes down.

The operation of this pulse can be misleading because the person feels and acts as though they are in the same place and that nothing is happening, and yet something is happening of which they are unaware. Suddenly, they may be up or down because the wave spikes or drops. It is the nature of the individual wave, like the breath. When we breathe in, we do not always anticipate when the end of the breath will be, nor can we anticipate that on the exhale, but we know that eventually, the turn happens. And it happens by its own nature and seemingly without any intervention from us.

As patients, these people can be very misleading. You can see them week after week after week, and they seem like they are in the same place. And then, very suddenly, they can go one way or another. That is why they are so explosive when it comes to illness. If you see an individual, especially one with an undefined Heart Center, you know they are building up for an explosion. That explosion can be a heart attack for them. They can look like everything is fine, and they are breathing fine, and everything is okay, and then 'bang.' [In more than fifty years of clinical practice, I have not had this experience, and the statistical data show that an undefined Heart Center does not predispose a person to have a heart attack.]

It is very important to recognize that the wave of an individually defined Solar Plexus Center person does not look like a wave. Think about the emotional movement of this wave; think about it in space moving so you see it as a spiral, and think about a slinky. One of the things that happen with individuals is that often, this wave gets compressed. The slinky gets tightened up. They get locked; that is what the plateau really is. They get locked at certain levels. You can end up with people who are chronically depressed and cannot get out. They get locked at that plateau. [We need to study this more to know if it is true.]

Breathing is of great importance in the life of these individually defined Solar Plexus Center people. Breathing opens up the slinky and stretches it so that its peaks and valleys are less and less extreme. Breathing and singing are very important for people with individual definitions because breathing opens up their energies and breaks the lock. [Anyone with Gate 12 does well to use breathing to balance their energy and to realign to their inner Self. I have validated this in my clinical practice. Ra is right about breathing and its importance.]

The Tribal Emotional Wave

The inside Channel between the Root Center and The Solar Plexus Center (Emotional System) is the Tribal wave. Gates 19, 49, 37, and 40 are part of these Channels. The Channel of Sensitivity operates in a normal, regular wave. The emotional wave is very reliable for this Stream. It operates like Ma and Pa kettle, where Pa can say, "Look out, it is the 28th of the month, and Ma is going to be in a lousy mood." It is as regular as clockwork.

Underlying this reliability is the Heart Center. Because the wave goes into the Heart Center (Ego) and not into the Throat Center (Thyroid) as the Abstract and Individual waves do, this wave gains regular support in a regular rhythm, which is what the tribe is all about. Waiting out this wave and its regular pattern is important for a person with this stream. This waiting honors the Authority of their emotional System and allows them to be healthy. Someone who has a definition but who does not honor this emotional Authority may develop kidney problems that occur on a regular basis. [This statement regarding kidney problems is unsubstantiated.]

People who have the Solar Plexus Center defined through these Channels go through a regular emotional wave. It is reliable. Unlike the other two streams, the tribal wave goes into the Heart Center and not into the Throat Center. The regularity of the heart allows for support that is part of the tribe's theme.

* * *

The Solar Plexus Center (emotional system) has these three different waves that impact how illness operates. If someone has a defined Solar Plexus Center (emotional system), they are tribal, they do not wait out their wave, tend to have ongoing problems with water retention, kidney problems, and lower back pain. In other words, the occurrence of the problem will be on a regular cycle. It will go away, and then it will come back again, and it will go away, and then it will come back again, etc.

The cycle will repeat itself, and, of course, it can become very serious. The problem will not just come and have its impact and leave. Jumping on a wave for these people rather than waiting out the wave and then deciding on things results in physical and emotional problems. It also may result in eating disorders. [We have no data on the medical aspects Ra is hypothesizing. From the data I analyzed, I did not find any correlation between what Ra said with medical data analyzed on 30,000 cases statistically and 15,000 cases clinically.]

When a person has an undefined Solar Plexus Center (emotional system) but has an activation in each of the three streams, they can be made ill in ways that do not belong to their Type and/or nature. They may pick things up from being in the aura of others and are vulnerable to taking those things into themselves. In

Design, we call this conditioning. [In the field of psychology and medicine, the term conditioning is very specific and variable. Ra's use of the term conditioning implies doing something based on outside rather than internal energy. Ra believed that humans have no choice. Data analysis shows that humans do have choices and that consciousness overrides conditioning.]

When you are dealing with a person with the defined Solar Plexus Center (emotional system), who is an individual, illness is a totally different story. These people can go along for many years while a disease is at work in them for all those years. And if you do not really look, you will never find it. Then, all of a sudden, the illness will peak, and it will come to the surface. That only happens if they are not paying attention to the authority that is there in their Solar Plexus Center (emotional system).

Finally, for the abstract person with the defined Solar Plexus Center (emotional system), an illness or disease has a quick onset. The illness plateaus fairly quickly, and then it is over quickly.

Most women with a defined Solar Plexus Center (emotional system) are not honoring their emotional authority, i.e., they do not wait out their wave and have ongoing problems with water retention and with their menstruation cycle. Most women who do not honor their Solar Plexus Center (emotional system) end up at some point or another with kidney problems. They also have lower back pain and lower kidney pain because the adrenal glands become stressed. If these people are jumping on the wave, they are always making the wrong decision. There is no truth in the now for anyone who has Solar Plexus Center (emotional system) definition, i.e., is emotionally defined. [It is essential to bring in data on the Four Worlds to consider how emotional energy can be transformed and aligned so illness does not surface. However, no medical data held up in the analyses we ran on 30,000 cases with five matched samples.]

On the other hand, when you are dealing with someone with an undefined Solar Plexus Center (emotional system) who has an activation in each of the three streams, they can be made ill. They can be made ill in a way that does not belong to them. For example, if they have a partner.

Whoever is abstract and loads up the abstract side is going to have a quick rise to the plateau and then a drop-down from it.

People with an undefined Solar Plexus Center (emotional system) do not get sick in the same way as people with a defined Solar Plexus Center (emotional system). People with an undefined Solar Plexus Center (emotional system) tend to get sick emotionally. They are the emotionally ill ones. The people with a defined Solar Plexus Center (emotional system) get ill physically, in their biology. Generally, that is the main difference between people with this Center defined or undefined. [This hypothesis is not substantiated.]

With the undefined Solar Plexus Center (emotional system), you are dealing with all kinds of emotional illnesses. The emotional illness then leads to the physical illness, which can be devastating if that person identifies with the emotional system. In other words, when someone identifies with the emotional system, emotional difficulty can then lead to some kind of physical problem. In most cases, these are people who begin to have real problems living in the world, and this is what the illness represents. These people may have real problems in making ends meet or real problems in maintaining relationships. Very often, they end up being the victims of violence or the perpetrators of violence. In domestic violence, the emotional wave may be exaggerated because undefined Solar Plexus Center (emotional system) people are living out somebody else's emotional wave. [These statements are Ra's speculation on how emotional energy affects people. His understanding of the psychological dynamics in emotional waves is limited, and he drew assumptions that have not been validated. When working with clients, it is important to use proper communication tools to unpack what is at work for that person before you make assumptions or put forth unsubstantiated hypotheses.]

People with an undefined Solar Plexus Center (emotional system) are very unstable in the nature of who they are. Whenever you are dealing with someone who is undefined in the Solar Plexus Center (emotional system), your first concern is for their emotional stability. Then, you can begin to help them. Until they recognize that all the guilt and blame and shame that they carry inside of them is not theirs, you cannot help them. The moment that they understand that all of that emotion is not their stuff, that the guilt has been placed in them, that all of those feelings have been put into them, and that they have been poisoned throughout their life by other people, that is the moment that they are liberated. It is the moment that they begin to see that they do not have emotional authority and that they cannot make decisions based on what they feel emotionally. That recognition is the beginning of making them healthy people, and that is where health starts. [Ra did not recognize the Four Worlds and how emotional energy must be transformed through the Emotional/Angelic World.]

The person with a defined Solar Plexus Center (emotional system) has physical illness, while the person with an undefined Solar Plexus (emotional system) has emotional illness. The two possibilities are very different. [Ra's hypothesis is unsubstantiated.]

Nervousness exists in the Solar Plexus Center (emotional system). As professionals, you will see everybody's stomach problems arising out of the Solar Plexus Center (emotional system) and not out of the Heart Center. The stomach is in the Heart Center itself. When you see someone with an undefined Heart Center, it is very important, depending on their Type, that they learn to re-evaluate their diet. You have to follow the Type in order to find out what diet is correct. Surprisingly enough, an undefined Heart Center is not an indication of difficulties in the stomach itself. The stomach, which is in the 40th Gate, is pointing to the mouth, which is in the 37th Gate. It is out of the Solar Plexus Center (emotional system) that the chemistry of the stomach is established. The Solar Plexus Center (emotional system) is where all the problems with the processing in the stomach come in.

If you are someone who has an undefined Solar Plexus Center

(emotional system), i.e., you are emotionally undefined, and you deal with emotional poisoning, there is a fundamental basic reaction. The stomach muscles tighten naturally, and discomfort occurs there; there is a potential for nausea and a throbbing in the body.

It can take 24 hours for those reactions to go away. That is really a long time for a reaction to clear from the body.

This open emotional system, the undefined Solar Plexus Center (emotion-al system), destroys the stomach. When a person identifies with the wave that comes into them, they start feeding on that wave, and it cannot pass out of their body. It affects the way in which the body vibrates on the inside, and it affects the stomach. It can release all kinds of acids into the stomach because this is where things like heartburn occur. Stomach difficulties are in the Solar Plexus Center (emotional system). An emotional wave can distort the proper operation of the stomach and lead to eating disorders. [Stomach problem causes include infections like H. Pylori, stress, dietary issues, allergies, and anatomical issues such as GERD. Before we accept Ra's hypotheses about the functioning of the digestive system, we need to collect data on different patterns. From the current statistical data, none of what is said about diet or medical conditions has been substantiated.]

The Root Center

Understanding the Root Center (Figure 17), its energies, and its formats is crucial in understanding some underlying themes in the other Centers. The Root Center is a very powerful Motor (Fuel). The pressure of the Root Center energies powerfully influences the nature of the way in which an individual expresses and experiences the stress or pressure that moves through them by being in the world. Energy cannot exist in the world without this pressure. Fear, stress, and pain make us human and drive our consciousness as fuels. These are the pressures and stress of being human.

> Actually, the need to achieve is the first primary pressure a baby experiences. It is the drive for competence, and without it, a baby would not survive. I disagree with Ra in stating that fear, stress, and pain make us human. These are emotions that drive some people, but many people are driven more by compassion, love, and service than by negative emotions.

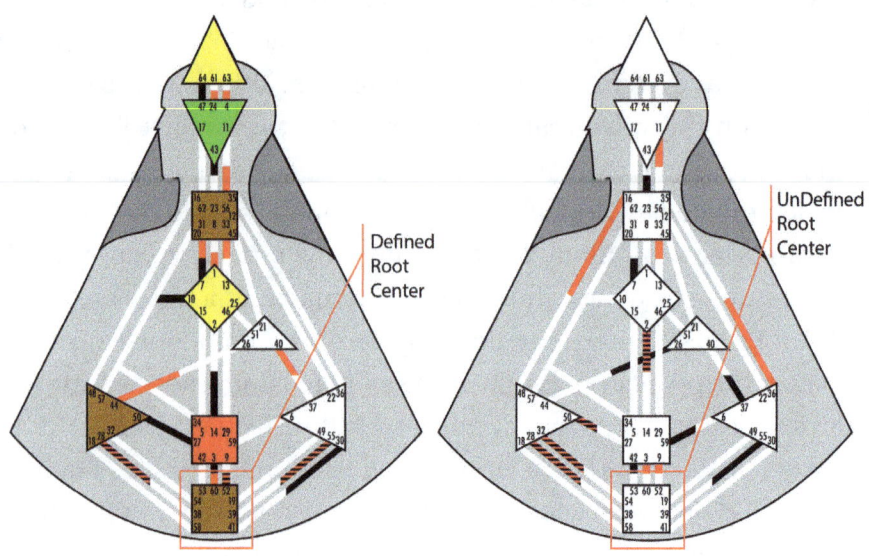

Figure 17: The Root Center

The Root Center has no direct access to the Throat Center but does have direct access to the Sacral Center. This is deeply significant because the Channels between the Root Center (adrenal, stress) and the Sacral Center are the format energies. The Root Center is a pressure center for the Sacral Center, the Splenic Center (immune system), and the Solar Plexus Center (emotional center), i.e., it fuels these centers. Basic pressures of life are created through the format energies, which are, therefore, critical in understanding the way pressures move and drive our consciousness. They are essential fuels for the whole living process.

Any definition or activation of format energy in a person tells you that that energy will deeply influence that person's expression of themselves in the world, i.e., how they handle the stress and pressures of being human.

> When Ra taught this class, he told Marvin and me that he based the formats on ideas from homeopathic principles. We have no data supporting Ra's assumptions, but the concepts are interesting and can be tested clinically in the field if you do readings.

The Root Center through the Format Energies

There are three different Formats (Figure 18). A Format may be Abstract, Individual, or Logical. Each Format relates to a different pattern and tells us a great deal about the way in which the person with that Format in their Design perceives and handles themselves. It is also important to know and understand your Format Energy pattern so you know how to handle yourself in times of illness and what kinds of vulnerability you have. [What Ra said about illness did not hold up statistically in any of the cases tested.]

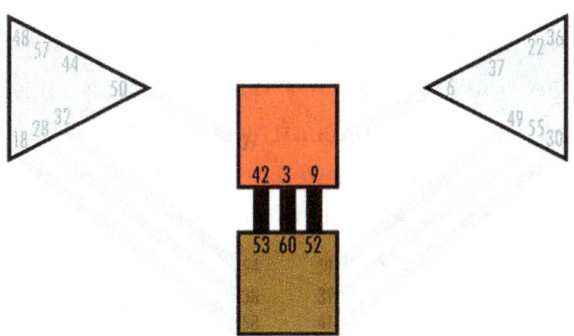

Figure 18: Format Energies

Abstract Format Energy: Gate 42 or Gate 53

Abstract format energy is cyclical. People who have abstract format energy get diseases that operate in stages. This energy has a beginning, a middle, and an end. In addition, it is a wet energy. People with this kind of Format are people who experience things in their life through cycles. They go through stages and must live through the whole cycle of a process in order for it to be completed. For example, someone with Abstract Format Energy who gets a cold goes through all the stages of the cold, from the sniffles to the full-blown runny nose, to a wet cough, to the resolution and finishing of the process. This cycle teaches the body something important for its integrity, and it lives out its own mechanical genetics in the cycle. People with the abstract format tend to have wet types of diseases, runny noses, pus, abscesses, etc. [This statement is unsubstantiated.]

As a professional, you can recognize when you see a Projector with Gate 42 or Gate 53 that the illness in them is already in one of its stages, and you may not be seeing it at the end of that stage. The illness is going to be on a cycle. The way to heal them is going to be in stages as well. A Manifestor can spontaneously heal. If they come for help, they can be healed very quickly. But, a Manifestor has to be able to ask for help.

Logical Format Energy: Gate 9 or Gate 52

The Logical Format energy is very focused. It is also dry. The person with a Logical Format is concentrated and the way in which they handle their lives is concentrated and focused, doing one thing at a time or going from one thing to another thing in a specific way. From the standpoint of disease, the person with a Logical Format gets ill with things that go deep and need powerful, concentrated medical treatment that is specific. You need to know exactly where the disease is focused, and you need to attack it directly and deeply for the healing process to occur. It is the same way with the Logical Format in any issue and area of life, i.e., Logical people go deeply into things and need to concentrate to get through them. [Again, these statements have no scientific documentation. I do know from my own Design with the Logical Format Channel 52-9 that I experience an inner sense of quiet and depth. However, I am exceptionally gifted at multi-tasking and can focus and do many things and handle many projects at the same time. This is contrary to what Ra is describing for this format type.]

Individual Format Energy: Gate 3 or Gate 60

Individual Format Energy operates in a pulse. It is the energy of mutation and change. It is not predictable in a consistent way because of its mutative capacity. It operates as the breath operates, in a pulse. People who have this Format have a deep melancholic aspect because, at some level of their being, they are in touch with the mutative nature of life itself and with its changing nature from moment to moment.

When an individual has Individual Format Energy, they must be careful when they get ill because the disease process can change easily from one form to another. With Individual Format energy, for example, an antibiotic that works for a day or two may stop working because the problem being treated or the organism being treated may mutate and need something different. People with Individual Format Energy need to be treated right away when they are ill; they cannot delay treatment because of their nature and the potential for mutation in their illness. A Manifestor who has the individual format energy and has a breast lump must be aware that the danger is that by the time they get into surgery, the problem may exist all over their body. They also tend toward depression because of their connection to the nature of mutation and change. For them breath and breathing are extremely important as a way to move them through their process and allow them to connect with their own essential nature. [Again, these statements are unsubstantiated. Because Ra stated that Channel 60-3 operates in a pulse, it makes sense to think that if this is true, it would be connected to the breath. Between the in-breath and the out-breath is a pause. Meditating on the pause connects you to higher consciousness and may be a powerful meditation. However, there is no data on how someone with this format responds to medications and no data on whether someone with Channel 60-3 is more prone to depression than someone with a different format. Do your own research. Be cautious in diagnosing or recommending medical care.]

In Hahnemann's homeopathic approach, these three format energies are matched by his three ways in which disease works. Classical homeopaths when they meet Human Design, and they understand the formats, are thrilled. They finally see what Hahnemann is talking about. He talked about the three ways in which disease and sickness operate. They operate with a wet cyclic, a mutative pulse, and focused dry format energy. It is also ancient medical knowledge, i.e., ancient Hindu Brahman knowledge and Indo-European knowledge, that came with the Chakra system a long time ago. This wet/dry concept is very important for healing.

The homeopathic field is moving away from one kind fits all. Homeopaths are beginning to understand that remedies relate to energy. All the official names of herbs are being changed because now it is all genetics. Scientists are finding that the herbs no longer can be talked about from the observational science of the 17th century. Herbs are all being renamed at the genetic level. That is so important because once we all get down to seeing a common denominator of understanding the way the mechanical things actually work, we will no longer have this broad brush that we put over everybody.

You can see, just at the surface of what we are looking at, how much more successful you can be with a patient just by recognizing how to deal with them. When you know that by seeing their Type and by seeing what is open in them, you can predict what kinds of difficulties they may face. You can look and see where the difficulty is going to be. If your patients can begin to experiment with their Type, your patient is on the path of well-being.

> Ra's interpretation of the format energies is interesting and may carry truth, but at this time, it is hypothetical and not verified. Thus, when dealing with clients, be cautious in using Ra's information on medical conditions or illnesses. Based on Marvin and my clinical data, relating format energies to physical conditions is premature and risky. Before using format energies medically, interview your client and learn about their history and treatments and how things actually work for them. Collecting data is critical in being a good clinician.

General Considerations

Knowing the Formats is essential in understanding how you operate in the world and knowing what kinds of things resonate with you. By knowing your Format, you may begin to understand your responses to people and to the world differently. In addition, you can use this information as a way to determine what kinds of treatments you may need when ill. [Ra was not medically trained; you are advised to consider your individual circumstances and seek qualified medical care rather than trusting that Ra's hypotheses are medically sound. None of Ra's statements about diseases and illnesses held up to statistical analysis on 30,000 cases and on more than 15,000 clinical cases.]

By having this kind of information, as a parent, you can also tailor treatment for your children according to their Format, Energy, and Type. A person with an Individual Format needs treatment and information right away before their issue mutates and they are in a different place altogether. The person with the Logical Format needs a focused approach and one that goes deep and precise. The person with the Abstract Format needs treatment or information that covers a spectrum and part of a cycle with closure on either end, i.e., they need to have the picture of the course their problem may take with the things to look for as well as the signs that will tell them the stage it is at in its cycle. As you begin to observe the way in which you and others respond to this kind of matched patterning, you may be very surprised at how basic and easy communication becomes and at how much more rewarding life feels. [Test Ra's hypotheses for yourself, and do not assume that they are true until you test them and do your own research.]

Remember that the Root Center is the basis of our pressure from below. It is the energy that fuels our Splenic, Sacral, and Solar Plexus Centers. It is powerful in setting the stage for many of the things in our lives. While the Root Center does not directly reach the Throat Center, it still determines a great deal about how those Centers function and how you function in the world.

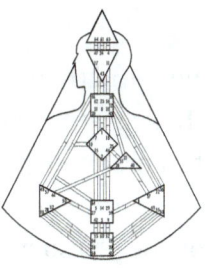

Overview of Profiles

Everyone comes into the world with a specific Profile (Figure 19) or purpose. Through this purpose, an individual can see how to attain fulfillment. Profiling is rooted in the understanding of the nature and structure of the hexagram, which is key to revealing an individual's genetic nature. A hexagram is built on six lines or six sub-themes. Each of these lines is an archetype within itself.

A hexagram can be seen as a metaphor for a house. At the base, the First Line forms the foundation. At the top, the Sixth Line is the roof. The house is a two-story house. The hexagram is divided into a lower trigram: the First Line, the Second Line, and the Third Line; and an upper trigram: the Fourth Line, the Fifth Line, and the Sixth Line.

The Human Design profile is derived from the individual body graph calculation. A fundamental duality governs programming: the duality of the Sun and the Earth. The Sun, through the neutrino stream, produces an ocean of programming that concretizes and grounds through the Earth.

Two calculations are part of the design: the Personality (the conscious aspect) and the Design calculation (the unconscious aspect). There is a Personality or conscious Sun and Earth in specific hexagrams and lines, and there is a Design or unconscious Sun and Earth in specific hexagrams and lines.

The Sun and Earth, both Personality and Design, represent 70% of who we are in terms of the nature of the themes of our programming. Through the lines of the Personality Sun/Earth (since they are opposite, they activate the same line number) and the line of the design Sun/Earth.

The profile, which is the conscious and unconscious Sun/Earth configuration, represents 70% of our program. The Sun produces 70% of the neutrino information, and the Earth transforms it. This profile is essential to read.

Only twelve structural profiles are possible: seven right-angle profiles, one juxtaposed profile, and four left-angle profiles. The seven Right Angle Crosses have the following profiles: 1/3, 1/4, 2/4, 2/5, 3/5, 3/6, 4/6. People with these right-angle profiles have a lower trigram personality. These people are not here to have transpersonal skills, and they are ill-equipped from the very beginning for that.

Whatever Right Angle Cross people meet in life has to come to them. The people with 1/3 and 1/4 profiles are inside themselves. The people with 2/4 and 2/5 profiles need to be called out. The people with 3/5 and the 3/6 profiles need to be bumped into to have something happen. All of the seven right-angle crosses are focused inward. This focus does not mean that people with these profiles are necessarily contemplative or introverted, that is not true. It means that they are inherently selfish in their own process. They are here to fulfill their own personal destiny. For them, life seems to be about them. They have a destiny that is fulfilled within themselves. It is not a destiny that they meet through the other. Right Angle Cross people are under enormous pressure to fulfill their lives within themselves.

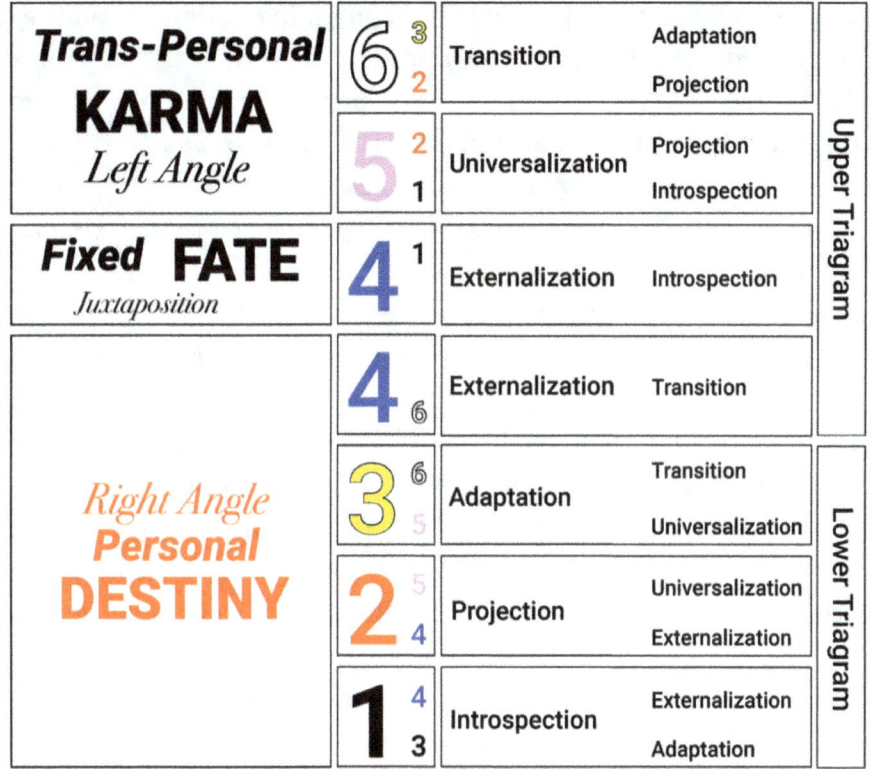

Figure 19: The Line Geometry Graph (Profile)

Right Angle Cross people, in psychological terms, can have numerous problems because their personality and their lower trigram lines focus all of their attention on themselves, on their own destiny. And yet, their unconscious is a transpersonal line. Their unconscious, the design part of their profile, is trying to grasp everything on the outside. They do not know why they get connected to people, nor do they understand their relationship to them. Their unconscious is looking to be pulled into the world, and their personality suffers. *Their unconscious pulls them into a process while their personality says, "But I am here for me, and I have to do my thing."*

The Juxtaposition Cross with the profile 4/1 is rare. There are not many people with this profile. This profile is all about fixed fate.

You can tell these are people about something in-depth, and they smile, and then they go home, and nothing changes. This means that if they say "no," this answer is a pure force, and they will go their way no matter what. *You cannot change the minds of people with 4/1 profiles. They are fixed individuals.*

The Four Left Angle Crosses have the following profiles: 5/1, 5/2, 6/2, and 6/3. These people have transpersonal karma. They know that nothing works without the other. They get fulfilled through the other. Their personality is upper trigram, but they all have an unconscious that is lower trigram. Thus, their personality is out there connecting with people because they are transpersonal, and their unconscious is always wanting to operate alone.

The Right-Angle Cross profiles show personal destiny, the 4/1 Juxtaposition profile shows fixed fate, and the Left-Angle Cross profiles show transpersonal karma. These terms can be very confusing because they can mean different things in different systems. In terms of the language of Human Design, these terms describe different Types of geometry. Fulfilling personal destiny creates enormous pressure for people who have the Right-Angle Cross profiles.

The picture is very different in the Left Angle Cross people who know that nothing works in their life without the other. Fixed Fate people do not let anything get in the way of their will, i.e., they can be destroyed, but they cannot be changed. These three basic themes of the three kinds of crosses are of tremendous value when looking at a patient's or a client's chart. You see quickly who is sitting in front of you and have a map of how that person operates in the world. You have a whole genetic view of the person you are dealing with, and then you can relate that to their specific Type, whether Manifestor or Generator, Projector or Reflector.

> The Voice did not give Ra information related to Profiles. In the statistical research on Profiles in 30,000 cases, the data showed that the Profile is a mathematical artifact of the structure of

the Astrological/Hexagram Wheel. Giving psychological meaning to a mathematical frequency does not stand up to scientific scrutiny. Because Profile did not hold up scientifically in the interpretive way Ra suggested, I delved into how the profiling patterns may be used more efficaciously.

The astrological wheel assigns each hexagram a set sequence, and each hexagram, with its lines, has a pattern of cosmic energy associated with it. Using the keywords related to the Sun/Earth axis in all time frames during early development, you can trace the movement of cosmic energy and its meaning during the first three months of life. In my clinical experience, using these keywords as an indicator of a person's issues and process yields a powerful tool for how an individual processes information and what and where they find the most growth.

I personally do not any longer use profile to describe someone as I find it formulaic, limiting, and disempowering.

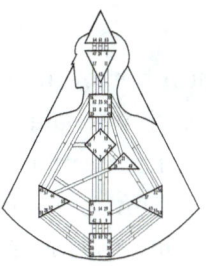

Looking at Lines

Medical Importance of Lines

When looking at a patient's or client's chart, it is important to remember that the profile tells about the purpose of that person's life. The profile gives an overview of a theme that carries throughout a person's life. [The keywords do this in a more empowering way than the lines, which are mathematical artifacts.]

First, use the four Gates of the profile within the medical matrix; second, use the line information. From these will emerge a significant theme about the person's health and diseases. Understanding the profile and the line basis, thus, becomes extremely important as a diagnostic tool. [When Ra refers to using the lines, go to the I-Ching and read the lines, or use the astrological degree and its nuance rather than profile.]

There are two important aspects to consider medically with respect to the lines. The first is the profile. The profile shows the purpose in life and gives an overview of a theme. [Use the Pattern of Orientation or The Cross information, as Ra calls it, to track the person's process. The tracking of a person's process is more powerful than looking at the mathematical artifact of the lines.]

Secondly, consider the number of activations in each of the six lines. The activation of lines shows balance and lack of balance that can be a real key to illness. The number of the lines activated also tells the impact of things. From these two aspects of design, you can understand, mechanically, the focus point in terms of how this person's health works and how this person can be best treated. We have no data on this process, but based on the statistics on illness in 30,000 cases tested, we did not find a correlation between illness and lines.

When you look at a chart in terms of lines, six different variations, depending on the line, reveal which medical aspects are likely in an individual with that configuration. The lines are a deep indication of the way in which the disease, or any kind of illness, is likely to operate. [This statement did not hold up statistically.]

Look at a person's chart and see how many lines they have in each of the six variations. The following pages will give you a general description of what each line means, followed by the medical aspects and health implications of the line.

Watching the lines is the most important thing in examining the health aspects of someone's chart. No matter what else you are looking at, whether it is Type, Centers, or Gates, watch the specific lines because they are always going to tell you about potential difficulties. [This statement is not supported.]

The Lower Trigram

> Ra's interpretation of the lines is hypothetical, not factual. When dealing with medical and psychological information, making the kinds of assumptions that Ra made about people ignores the complexity of how information is coded and processed on an individual basis. We now know that individuals are impacted by their biology, as in DNA, their epigenetic inheritance, and their emotional inheritance.
>
> The complexity of the medical and psychological issues for

> an individual is far greater than line analysis. In fact, none of the diseases or illnesses that Ra associated with Lines were statistically significant in 30,000 cases. Read over this section and use it by looking at a specific Hexagram, its astrological meaning, and its line meaning in the I-Ching. Once you do your research and take a history from your client, use your judgment about drawing any medical or psychological conclusions.

First Line

General Aspects: The First Line is the line of introspection. It is the foundation. First Line themes are about looking inward, trying to solve the basis of things. The First Line person has poor transpersonal skills and is very self-involved. The First Line person is the investigator, always trying to find out the real foundation of things. The First Line represents the essence of the Gate's theme. Wherever a person has First Line themes, it becomes imperative for them to find out what the basis is of that Gate, what the foundation is.

Medical Aspects: Because the First Line is introspective, illnesses or diseases connected to the First Line can be deep within the foundation and may never come out. A serious problem may exist, but the person with a First Line theme does not really know it is there. The problem is deep down underneath. Hypochondria can be associated with that because the First Line is always looking deeper and is introspective. Thus, the First Line person can have this sense that there may be something wrong here or there. It is deep. It is below the surface. It is inside. It is not known or necessarily visible on the outside.

Here, as a professional, you are dealing with insecurity. The insecurity may be inferiority or uncertainty. The insecurity in the First Line may be based on something mechanical or psychological. In someone carrying a First Line somewhere in their design, there may be an inherent weakness in an associated organ that the First Line reveals. [The First Line is also the Foundational Line. It may indicate strength as much as introspection. Be discerning and tread cautiously in this hypothetical area.]

Because the first Lines generally mean the basis, the foundation, and introspection, it is important to understand from a diagnostic point of view that you are looking at the potential for what insecurity in that line can mean.

In the genetic continuity of all First Lines lies inferiority. It is a basis on which to build superiority. You do not become introspective and seek out the foundation unless you feel like you do not have the foundation. A person with First Lines can end up with many disturbances rooted in that principle.

For example, a person who has Line 1 in the 40th Gate, the stomach, may show an inability or insecurity in their stomach. Their stomach may show uncertainty as to whether or not it can actually handle or properly deal with what is going on. The presence of Line 1 may tell you, the professional, that this inability is based on a biological fact. Line 1 tells you, alerts you, that there may be a problem in this area and that you need to look into it and do the research. [We have no verification of this hypothesis.]

Second Line

General Aspects: The Second Line is a binary to the First. In a sense, it is almost the opposite. The Second Line is the main floor of the story. It is at street level with the windows looking out onto the street. The Second Line is a line of projection. It is the projection that comes from the outside. The Second-Line theme is about going about your own business and not really wanting to be involved with what is going on on the outside. The Second-Line person is quite content to be occupied within oneself.

The Second-Line theme is like a person who is naked walking around in their house at night, with the lights on. There are all kinds of people walking by on the street who can look in. Second-Line people are always seen, and they are always being called out. It is the theme of the Second-Line person to recognize that they are here to wait for the call. When the call comes, only then is there the opportunity to successfully go out from one's world and enter into something new.

Medical Aspects: Because a person with Line 2 is busy living their life and is occupied within themselves, other people need to see when this person is sick. It is as simple as that. Other people come up to this person and say, "are you ok - is something the matter?" The Second-Line person is very self-absorbed, they are doing their own thing, and they do not do research. These are the kind of people who can walk around half-blind and not realize it until someone says to them, "I thought you could read that sign." They assume that no one can read that sign. Or they are sitting six inches from the television to see, and they assume that everyone else sits that close, too. They think something is normal until someone points it out to them that it is not.

Line 2 is about denial. Denial is an important theme because it means, "when you are meeting denial," you are not meeting revealed symptoms. There is a block there. For example, clotting in the blood, aneurysms, that kind of thing could easily be a Second-Line theme. The Second Line is all about denial. Refusing to see and refusing to hear can be part of the Second-Line theme; thus, denial can lead, particularly, to blindness and deafness.

Wherever you look at Second Lines in a design, there will either be a mechanical thing that you see, or there will be a Second-Line issue which will end up as part of the personality construct. Whenever you are looking at the Second Line, you can always see that there is the potential for a real problem there. The problem is rooted in denial. When you are dealing with a Second-Line personality, you will often have people who deny needing help. They may not tell you they need help until it is too late.

In other words, it is very important with a Second-Line child to realize that you need to see when they are sick. You cannot expect them to notice that they are sick; they may not notice.

Looking at the design, at each of the Gates where the lines have activations, when you see them this way, especially as a professional, you get an extraordinarily profound picture of what is going on for a person on many levels.

By looking at the lines in different places in this language, the total make-up in the person begins to emerge, to become clear. Looking at the lines in this way is like putting things under the microscope. The next level of Keynotes can be called Medical Keynotes. As a professional, you can begin to look at the lines with an easy perspective. You are not just dealing with the lines as a psychological language used in doing analysis, but now you can begin to put them in medical terms.

To see that the Second Line can mean something totally different, we will look at an example of the role of sexuality. Gate 59, Line 2 (59.2) is shyness. This is also the denial of the ability to give birth. The meaning may be psychological, but it could also be physical. When you see that, you know that it is either one or the other. It is just a matter of strategy; the Second-Line strategy is, "You have to come to me and call me out," or it is a physical reluctance to be called out.

Through the Second Line, you set up a barrier that can be selective. In other words, it only lets in a certain molecule but does not let in another. This kind of denial can really be seen as some kind of blockage or filtering system. The filtering can be positive, but if that Second Line was in the Solar Plexus Center, the filtering could also indicate problems in the kidneys.

A patient with a Second Line that indicates a problem in the kidneys would be a patient who was not going to be sensitive to their problem until it got to the point where it was so obvious that they had to deal with it. Kidney disease is often intrinsically insidious until dialysis or some other major intervention is necessary anyway. But there are people who all of a sudden appear, their body has swollen up, and they are in kidney failure. These people could easily be Second-Line people with Solar Plexus Center activation.

Also, people with First, Second, and Third Lines lack transpersonal skills.

These are not people who naturally turn to others for help.

> No correlations between illness and Lines were significant in research on 30,000 cases or on more than 15,000 clinical cases.

Third Line

General Aspects: The Third Line is the line of adaptation. The Third Line is inherently unstable. It is unstable because it is a transition place between the First and the Second floor of the house. It is where the stairway is. It is the final stage in the personal experience. The Third Line, the line of adaptation, is about trial and error. It manifests as a life of bumping into things and having things bump into you. The First three lines, being self-absorbed, are not prepared for the other. The Third-Line person who is being bumped into is surprised and has to learn how to adapt. The Third Line person has to learn how to meet the other. Through this process of trial and error, somewhere down the road lies a potential for wisdom.

Medical Aspects: Third-Line people are people who are always being infected. They are always getting bumped from the outside. They are always unprepared. Someone takes a Third-Line person outside, and they catch a chill. It is that kind of thing. The Third-Line person goes outside feeling terrific, gets unexpectedly kissed, and six days later, they are sick. It is very typical for Third-Line people to constantly have things bump into them. Being open, it becomes dangerous. After a while, the Third-Line person starts to feel that they do not want anyone to come near them.

Because they are so open, the Third-Line person can be very physically disturbed by other people. They never know what will bump into them, so there is no protection. For this reason, they can use avoidance as a strategy in their lives.

The Third-Line is pessimism. The nature of pessimism is that "things do not work as they should." Because of the nature of trial and error, the presence of the Third Line means that there will be unpredictable things at work. The Third Line is the most mutative line at the medical level. Consequently, Third-Line people are the most susceptible to bumping into things that other people would most likely not meet. They get bizarre infections from the middle of the jungle, where everyone else gets a mosquito bite. It is possible for them to bump into the unusual in that sense.

Third-Line pessimism is very strong at the psychological level. Third-Line people have a sense that what is best can never be achieved.

When you are dealing with a Third-Line theme medically, you need to understand that things are not necessarily going to look like what you expect. Things look different because the Third Line has a mutative potential to it. Thus, only through the Third Line are we able to adapt through our immune system. The Third Line is a line of adaptation.

One of the things about the Third Line being is that often, illness provides an opportunity for others. In other words, if you have a whole bunch of Third-Line people, and they are all infected with a killer disease, out of them all, there will be one of those Third-Line people who has a natural immune protection to the disease. You will not find this in any other line. This is the value of the Third Line.

Professionally, you are going to meet many people who do not have any Third Lines in their design.

In diagnosing patients, it is very important to have information visible that shows exactly which planets are in which lines. From this information, you can see the areas with inferiority problems right away and where the uncertainty is. The computer program for printing design charts has this essential feature.

To summarize the lower trigram, let's look at a few examples: if you see a person who has Saturn in the second Gate, Line 1, you know that this person is very uncertain about direction. This person will feel very uncomfortable about where they are going and where they might go. If you have someone with Mars in the 50th

Gate, Line 2, you know their denial is about values. But more than that, Gate 50 is a primary immune Gate. The Line 2 denial may be blocking what they need in order to operate their immune system successfully. You can go through the lines and see them like this.

When looking at a patient's lines, have the information up on your computer screen. When someone comes to you with kidney problems, look first at the Solar Plexus Center (emotional system) because that is natural. Then, look further to see what Gates in the Solar Plexus Center (emotional system) is being defined. Next, look at what the lines are. You are actually going to be able to see which Gate and which line is specifically responsible for your patient's problem. To start with, look at your own design this way and the designs of members of your family.

> Be cautious when interpreting charts this way because there is no data supporting what Ra said about illness and diseases. In fact, all of his statements on Gates, Lines, and Centers associated with diseases did not hold up statistically despite numerous iterations with the data.

The Upper Trigram

The upper trigrams, Lines 4 through 6, are transpersonal in nature. People with these lines are best equipped to deal with each other, and they are fulfilled through their interaction with each other. They have a transpersonal need to be fulfilled through their communion with others, unlike the lower trigram people, who are self-absorbed and preoccupied with their own personal destinies. The Fourth-, Fifth-, and Sixth-Line people look towards the other, and through that connection with the other, they look for fulfillment in their own process.

The upper trigram has real thematic changes. The Fourth, Fifth, and Sixth Lines are inherently transpersonal. Lines 1, 2, and 3, in terms of disease, point to inherited disease. Inherited diseases are unlikely in people with the Fourth, Fifth, or Sixth Lines. What you find in people with Lines 4, 5, and 6 are transmitted diseases. Look into family histories and find kidney problems in the family. You are going to be interested in the first three lines because they are going to be the indication of the movement of that disease. Above that, Lines 4, 5, and 6 show transmitted diseases because they are transpersonal by nature. Lines 4, 5, and 6 relate to diseases that actually require a living host to pass on the disease rather than the disease being transmitted genetically through the line itself. Diseases of Lines 4, 5, and 6 require a transpersonal host. There will be those people who host a disease and those who pass it on.

4 Fourth Line

General Aspects: The Fourth Line is deeply fixed. It is fixed on its own point of view. It is, after all, the foundation of the second floor of the house. It is the externalizing of the foundation. The externalizing of their fixed perspective occupies Fourth-Line people throughout their lives. The key

To their success in life, they are able to establish fruitful relationships and, through these friendships, have the opportunity to get the ear of the other.

Medical Aspects: These are the infectors. The fourth Line externalizes; it is its job. The Fourth-Line person can influence the well-being of others. But because they are opportunistic in their design, they get diseases that operate in those rare moments of opportunity. Fourth-Line people are people who get very funny things. They go on a sightseeing tour of Mexico, and they end up getting some parasite inside of them that finds its one opportunity in the Fourth-Line person.

But this dynamic works both ways with Fourth-Line people. They can also bring disease to others because they are natural externalizers, e.g., the Fourth-Line child who has a cold can infect their whole class. The Fourth Line is a line of influence. Fourth-Line people are necessary to make sure that the ongoing immune system, the total immune system, of our species stays healthy.

When the Fourth-Line person gets something, they give it to everybody else so that the others' immune systems can also take it in and work with it.

The Fourth Line can be influential in a very frightening way. It can bring death and destruction, yet because we do not see things from the proper perspective, it can also bring long-term immunity.

For their personal well-being, Fourth-Line people have to be careful about those moments when the opportunity is on the other side of them. They get the rarest things. As a doctor dealing with a Fourth-Line person, you try to figure out what is wrong with them; you have all these basic mundane directions that are being pointed at, but the chances are that, with a Fourth-Line person, it is something much more obscure. What the Fourth-Line person has may not necessarily be in the literature or the usual literature because what they have is going to be something unusual.

The theme of the Fourth Line is exhaustion; it can be debilitating.

The classic Gate for exhaustion is the 30th Gate, Fourth Line, which is called "Burn out." So, anything that becomes obsessive to someone with this line can lead to complete exhaustion. If this person becomes an obsessive golfer, instead of becoming healthy, the golf becomes exhausting and depletes the person's resources.

The 56th Gate, Fourth Line, is exhaustion from overstimulation. This is a mental process; too many ideas and too many things need to be dealt with, which always leads to exhaustion. The 56th Gate describes an over-taxing of the mind.

The presence of many Fourth Lines in a person's design may mean that the person uses up an extraordinary amount of energy. The Fourth-Line is by far the most influential line. It is probably the greatest carrier or host for transmitting diseases. It is single-pointed. It is fixed. It can be very obsessive. Wherever you see the presence of the Fourth Line, recognize that this is a place of potential deep exhaustion, psychologically as well as physically.

Obsessive-compulsive disorders are partially inherited and partially transmitted. A person with an obsessive-compulsive disorder might have an upper/lower trigram mixed profile. They often might have a 1/4 or a 2/4 profile. The insecurity that makes a person move to a ritualistic obsession is very draining. That insecurity can never be satisfied.

5 Fifth Line

General Aspects: The Fifth Line is always subject to the projection of others. Others anticipate that Fifth-Line people can perform better than anyone else can. The assumption by the other is that the Fifth-Line person has the capacity to universalize and will not fail. The Fifth Line often brings deep dilemmas in terms of reputation.

Like its parallel harmony to the Second Line, the Fifth Line is the second-floor window. The lights are not on. They are off. Rather than the Fifth-Line person being seen from the outside, the Fifth-Line person is the one who is watching. The Fifth-Line person looks out of the window, and down below, those who are walking by do not really know if there is anyone up there. There is the projection. What is in the room? Who could be there?

The fifth-Line person is always dealing with the question of reputation. When the fifth-Line person can bring what is practical and universalize what is practical, then the projection of the fifth-Line person grows and expands. There is a glow to the reputation. When the fifth-Line person cannot deliver, when that person cannot bring what is practical, reputation suffers in that moment.

Medical Aspects: Moving from the Fourth Line to the Fifth Line brings something new. The nature of the Fifth Line is that it is the only exalted line in the I-Ching. The Fifth Line carries specific responsibilities. It is looked up to in terms of the hexagram. The Fifth Line is expected to deliver the goods now that the process is complete. Consequently, the Fifth Line is always being projected upon as someone who can bring practical solutions. The Fifth Line is the line of the saint, the savior, the general, and the heretic, all of these things.

When you look at the Fifth Line from a medical standpoint, one of the things to pay attention to is that the keynote for this line is paranoia. It is very important to understand the power of that paranoia. It is the capacity of the Fifth Line to be able to universalize. The Fifth-Line person, when paranoid about something, has the ability to sound the alarm if they see that the paranoia is legitimate. But because heretics get burnt at the stake, the Fifth-Line person, when sounding an alarm, must always make sure that the alarm has a solid basis under it.

The Fifth Line is about universalization. It is rooted in projection. Fifth-Line people are basically the healthiest of all beings. Whenever you look at a Fifth-Line person, you are looking at the potential for well-being. But because the Fifth-Line person is the subject of others' projections, others can bring the Fifth-Line person to illness. However, this is very unusual.

Many people project on the Fifth-Line person that they are healthy or not healthy. The more a lack of health is projected on them, the unhealthier they become. Not every Fifth-Line person will know that this projection is just part of the mechanics.

The Fifth-Line person does not want to have their reputation hurt. The Fifth-Line person who has friends who say, "You shouldn't be doing that," or "You shouldn't be doing this, and it's not good for you," may end up changing their basic diet or their habits and then get sick. Not every Fifth-Line person has the capacity to consider that kind of pressure lightly and to stay centered within their own nature.

Most importantly, at another level, the fifth-Line person has the opportunity to inform everybody else about the presence of disease. It is one of their gifts. The Fifth-Line person has the capacity to call people and let them know what is going on.

Fifth-Line people often cry wolf. It is not like all Fifth-Line people are going to be terrific. Sometimes, they really do cry wolf and say,

"There is a problem with this," or " There is a problem with that." It is similar to all those Fifth-Line people who got carried away by bizarre diseases in Africa. The power of projection in the Fifth-Line person tries to get everybody terrified.

Most Fifth-Line people, regardless of whether the Fifth Line is in their personality (conscious) or design (unconscious), have their reputation as a major concern in life. It is essential for them to withdraw from the pressures of the community, often because they are uncomfortable with scrutiny. Most Fifth-Line people do not like doctors. They do not like the fact that somebody is going to project onto them. They would rather feel comfortable, know it themselves, and become doctors themselves than they can tell other people about it. These are people who will not let you know they are ill. They hide their illness.

The secret is that it is the Fifth-Line people who bring practical solutions to disease. Fifth-Line people also get practical diseases. They do not get the weird stuff like the Fourth-Line people do. They are going to get to the common ground because they are really the call of the common voice. They get those things that are prevalent. So, a Fifth-Line person gets a prostate infection.

Prostate infection is the biggest news in America. It is a practical disease. It is a practical warning to the people of this nation. Prostate infections are a universalized theme now. There is endless prostate advertising. It says something about how society functions and what people in society eat. It is typical of the Fifth Line. It is practical in the sense that it can be healed practically. We already know what to do with it. We do not know how to get rid of it, but we know how to heal it. [I did research on Fifth-Line men to determine if Ra's statement about the prevalence of prostate infections being more common among Fifth-Line men than other men was valid. The presence of the Fifth Line did not show significance in differentiating men with prostate infections.]

The Fifth Line brings these practical solutions. The gift of the Fifth-Line person is to bring solutions. It is important to grasp that people get diseases where they are vulnerable. In the Human Design system, the vulnerability lies in the undefined Centers. People are especially vulnerable when they identify with their undefined Centers.

It is very difficult not to identify with a person's emotional field and emotional tensions. Only when a person comes to understand their design and how their mechanics work can they truly begin to live a healthy life.

The mad scientist in his laboratory, who is a Third-Line person, may be able to discover something, but it is the Fifth-Line person who gets the world to know that something has to be dealt with. Aids would have begun with a Fourth-Line person, but a Fifth-Line person would recognize it. The Fifth-Line person will say there is something wrong with that. The reason that the Fifth-Line person will say that is because that person is open and susceptible to taking that in.

The Fifth-Line person can be very vulnerable to infection and has a good reason for being paranoid. They have within them the potential to come up with practical solutions. Old wives tales, your great grandmother's remedy, was looking at Fifth-Line things. They recognized a problem and stayed withdrawn during that time, and then, they were able to come up with solutions. They could begin to see what was practical. They found out that this leaf or this herb, or this tea was a remedy to a problem.

It is important to distinguish medically between the profile, which is the purpose in life and can give us an overview of a theme, and the number of activations in the six lines. Medically, the number of activations in the six lines is much more important to look at. From the line activations, you will be able to see when things are unbalanced and all of that. That becomes a real key. The lines give you the impact.

As a professional, if you look at someone's chart, if you just look at the Fifth Lines, every one of those Fifth Lines tells you where that person is open (vulnerable) to infection. The Fourth Line can put the disease out. It indicates a stronger immune ability than the Fifth Line, which shows susceptibility to infection. In other words, the best defense is a good offense.

6 Sixth Line

General Aspects: The Sixth Line is the roof of the house. It is not really a part of the hexagram at all. In a sense, it is the judge of whether or not the hexagram operates properly. It sits above everything. The Sixth Line is the line of transition, and it is the line of aloofness, climbing up to the roof of the house, not being involved, but being an observer, a recluse, and the fool on the hill. Watching. It is the Sixth Line that brings validation to the themes of the hexagram.

The real dilemma for a Sixth-Line person is to finally commit to what they recognize as correct rather than simply being the observer. When the sixth-Line person can come down off the roof, help, and get involved, then the sixth-Line person completes their process. Sixth-Line people then leave their aloofness behind and enter into a period of transition, where they recommit to the dynamic process of life.

Medical Aspects: It is very important to understand the Sixth Line technically. The Sixth-Line person lives through three different themes in their life. These themes are precise. The Sixth-Line person in the first 28.6 years, the Saturn cycle, lives out, essentially, a Third-Line theme. Optimism is the theme of the Sixth Line. This theme is the harmony of the Third-Line theme of pessimism. It is very important. This is another mutative capacity.

The Sixth-Line person is not the same as the Third-Line person because the Third-Line person's mutative quality is very powerful and is about adaptation. The theme of the Sixth-Line person is to be aloof.

Sixth-Line people get sick when they are young. Sixth-Line children get leukemia. These are the "good die young." By the time the Sixth-Line person gets to their Saturn return, they get to the period of their aloofness. They climb up to the roof of the house. They become a true Sixth-Line person then.

Sixth-Line people get illnesses when they are young, in the first period. They may end up spending the rest of their life separate from others in hospitals, in wheelchairs, and in institutions. They can carry early-life diseases for the rest of their life.

In the process of the Sixth-Line person, only when they get to a certain point can they be engaged. The Sixth-Line person always begins as pessimistic. If they do not get a disease by the time they are 28.6 years old, they are not going to get one. This is all about childhood diseases. It is also about the actual birth and creation of brand-new childhood diseases, where the Sixth-Line person before their Saturn return can be vulnerable to them. This is mutative.

If Sixth-Line people are lucky in those first 28.6 years, they do as all Sixth Lines do. After that, they rise above whatever is around them. They become aloof and distant. They separate themselves.

It is very important as a professional that when you see a child with a Sixth-Line theme in their profile, you know right away that they are going to be very vulnerable in those first 28 years. These children are the ones that you have to keep track of because they are in a very dangerous period of their lives.

These Sixth-Line people go through the next twenty-year time span, from 28.6 years to the Chiron return, approximately 51 years, when they are aloof. During this twenty-year time period they are fundamentally healthy. But, if they got some disease or illness in the first part of their process, they would live with it throughout their aloofness. In other words, they may be in a wheelchair for the next twenty years, but they are not going to get sicker. It is an interesting thing about it. This twenty years for the Sixth-Line person is a period of withdrawal, and nothing new is going to happen to them during that time. They become quite distant in that time, psychologically as well as physically.

What is interesting about the Sixth-Line people is that they are the ones who get sick young and the ones who get sick old. They have that period between 28.6 and 51 years when they are basically healthy.

It is important not to frighten people with this information. But it is very common for Sixth-Line people to die young. They may die in their early sixties. What happens to them is after the Chiron phase, they have to go back into the world. They cannot be aloof anymore. At that time, their immune system no longer protects them. Their immune system keeps them on guard during the middle twenty-year span. But by the time they get to the Chiron return, they are driven back into the world.

Sixth-Line people are probably the source genetically of what we call Alzheimer's. We probably will be able to find that out at some point because they are the ones who bring this return to an early cycle in life again. This relates to old cliché about becoming the child again, because they have to come off the roof and go back into the world. The disease that these Sixth-Line people most often get is the disease of being a child again, i.e., deterioration that takes place, which we call senility or Alzheimer's. [There is no evidence to support this hypothesis, and projecting this kind of interpretation may be damaging to your clients.]

In saying such a thing, about those configurations, remember, it is always important to look at a person's design and many other things as well. There is a memory circuit that runs through the whole body. If you have somebody who is a Sixth-Line person and they have a strong memory circuit, you know that they are not going to become senile. In other words, it is going to manifest as something else.

What is important for the Sixth-Line people to know is that this period of aloofness gives them a false sense of security. "Yes, I got polio when I was a kid." Polio was very common in the fifties generation. Sixth-Line kids got polio. And then they go through that twenty years until they are 50 years old and they have dealt with it. They say, "It is okay, I am actually very healthy." And then they get post-polio syndrome or whatever. Suddenly, they get to that point in their life where they really thought they had survived it, handled it and did really well. They have been in a long-term remission.

When you look at someone's design and see the Sixth-Line, you need to care for and nurture this person properly for the first part of their life. They need to have the good luck to have shelter and medicine. They are the most vulnerable of any other line profile during that period of their life (until they are 28.6 years old).

Optimism is what holds these people together. When you are dealing with someone who has cancer and is a Sixth-Line person, use this line of knowledge to give them the inner courage that they need to generate the optimism that things will really work for them. They will respond to this encouragement.

As an example, let us say that a person only has one Sixth Line and it is the Sixth Line of the 30th Gate. You know from this information that the only way you are going to reach them is through feelings (Gate 30). You are only going to be able to contact the optimism in them through the way in which you share your feelings with them and get them to reciprocate. They may have the Sixth Line in the 62nd Gate. Then, the only way to get to them is through the facts and details (Gate 62). And it is the facts that will give them optimism. Use the line information combined with Gate information to communicate with your patients in ways they can understand and relate to.

Learning to communicate with your patients through understanding their lines and how they relate on a cellular level will be extremely helpful. If a Third Line patient is sick, and you say to them, "Look, I do not know if I can help you, we can try some things." Because the Third Line is about pessimism, your statement absolutely satisfies them. When a Sixth-Line person comes to see you, if you say, "This is what we have and how we treat your illness, and it is certainly going to work," they will be hopeful and optimistic. Each line needs a different approach and different nuances of communication.

> Working with Lines at this point in the research on Human Design is premature since they are a mathematical artifact in how they function in a person's chart. More specifically, using the astrological sign and its dwad or undercurrent of nuanced meaning may yield more specific information that may be more accurate. Since none of the medical or illness data that Marvin and I analyzed showed statistical significance, read what Ra wrote and use it cautiously and with great care about the consequences to your clients with misinformation that relates to their health and well-being. I personally use the meaning of the Lines in the Trigrams of the hexagram and do not generalize about lines. I find it more powerful to look at the cosmic energy of the hexagram and the sequence of hexagrams and their meaning in Noble Energy Maps® in the Four Worlds.

There are different ways to deal with people. This is a very simple, basic guide for each of the six lines. As a professional, if you are dealing with a Second-Line person who is in denial, you just know that no matter what you say to them, they are denying that it will work. Do not be disturbed by that because that is their way.

If you have a First-Line patient, say to them, "Here is a journal about your disease, go read about it. Go do your research." They are going to feel terrific. They are so uncertain about what the disease is and who the doctor is, and they are asking, "Do they really know their stuff?" They need to find out. So, this First-Line person is the type of patient to whom you give the latest research information so they can read it themselves. Then they come back, and you can both have an intelligent conversation about what you do together in the process. We have already looked at the Sixth-Line person who needs something to find hope in, something to be optimistic about.

> Do your own research and keep notes on your client's verification of your statements.

Watching Transits as a Healthcare Care Professional

The most essential transit to watch with patients is the line transit. This is the most important thing. When you have a patient who comes to you on a First-Line Day, you are not really going to get to the bottom of things. If you were really going to run a practice properly, you would only work on Fourth- and Fifth-Line days. You would only have people come in at those times because that is when they are ready to get things out, when they are open to practical solutions, and when they are open to relating on a transpersonal level to the other. On a First-, Second-, and Third-Line Day, you have patients who are going to be closed off. In a Third-Line person, you have to penetrate them. If they are a Second-Line person, you have to call them out. It does not mean that they are necessarily responding to you.

This information helps to form a concrete, logical basis on which everyone can be treated properly. This is translatable information. It gives a manual, a floor plan, so that any doctor or health care professional can see the A, B, and C of it. By the time the place of disturbance in the body can be identified and the Line can be seen, not only do you know what you have to deal with, but you will also know how to deal with the person.

Everything about this information is about its transpersonal power. The moment you are aware and you can make someone else aware of their nature, that is when you can do something with them. It is the time when they can really be helped.

It is very exciting to see all the therapeutic applications. But eventually, none of these therapeutic applications will ever be used. Eventually, society will get to a point where children are raised according to design information. [Noble Energy Maps® show how babies are impacted by cosmic energy from three months before birth until three months after birth, as their primary experience of where and how energy coming from outside affects them. During this critical period of development, babies learn to know who they are internally and gain a strong sense of what aligns and does not align with them. Knowledge about how we all live in Four Worlds that come together, giving us the inner experience of ourselves, is available through Noble Sciences and my work.] Society will get to the point of not dealing with the victims of conditioning who come in their mid-life to try to find out who they are and then need to deal with the psychological dilemmas.

The foundation that is really being established with this information is for parents so they can understand their children. It is for doctors so they can understand their patients. It is for educators so they can understand their students. It is for employers so they can understand their employees. And on and on, so that we all can have a really deep respect for each other based on our design.

The most important thing to remember is that each and every individual is unique. To have a blueprint of this uniqueness is extremely valuable and necessary in order to communicate with that person as well as to treat that person. Think of the different automobiles that are on the market. There are so many different types and styles, shifts, and automatics; the differences are endless. You would never expect your mechanic to tune- up your BMW as he would a Ford Mustang. A Cadillac is not a Volkswagen.

The same is true for human beings. Each human being is in a different body. It is their vehicle in this life. Healthcare professionals who can learn how to distinguish these differences in dealing with their patients and their clients will be doing a tremendous service to the evolution of civilization.

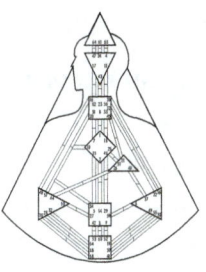

Closing

From this introduction, you have learned some of the language of Design and its usefulness. Knowing your Type is the first step in learning to live true to your Design. Once you know your Type, you can learn and understand the nuances of the Centers and gain increased awareness of the mechanics of Design. We have reviewed all Nine Centers and looked at their primary role in your Design and your Health. You have gained an insight into the mechanics of energy in your body and your being and have begun to recognize and understand your own nature.

You can use Design to know when you are living in a way that is true to you or not. Your awareness through Design can enhance your honesty in your own reactions through your awareness of entering into things in the way that is correct for you. After all, there is no right or wrong in the absolute. There is only what is or is not right for an individual, given the context and the circumstances surrounding them and the event. Design is a no-fault system that is logical and empirical. By understanding and knowing your own mechanics, you have the map of your nature through which you can be yourself, and when being yourself, you are who you are. You cannot and should not attempt to be other than that. Perfection exists in life itself, and as you come into your own fullness of life as you are designed to live it, you experience your own true perfection and that of others.

This exploration is very profound and goes deeper the more you explore. It has proved itself to be fruitful for many people around the world already, and they are learning about their mechanics every day. We have committed ourselves to facilitating the exploration of Design because we know its value and its benefit for the future of all generations. Join us in the exploration by beginning the experiment of living your Design. Experience the changes in yourself and those around you. Be yourself. Love Your Self.

> As you can see from reading through this book, Ra covered a lot of ground, and he delivered it in a wonderfully woven tapestry of information that touched deeply on many areas we all experience. My commentaries about the statistical and clinical research that spanned nearly thirty years fulfill my contract with Ra Uru Hu to keep myself outside of the Human Design Community while gathering the clinical and scientific data to put this work on a solid scientific foundation.
>
> Although I did not understand what I was doing while researching and clinically working with the Noble Energy Maps®, I recognize retrospectively that Human Design and Noble Energy Maps® validate that human beings live in multiple dimensions: the Mental/Waking, Emotional/Angelic, Spiritual/Archetypal, and Physical/Biological Worlds. (The body map statistics and the Four Worlds statistics validate the body maps and their accuracy psychologically and developmentally). The Worlds come together when a baby is three months old, forming an integrated consciousness that drives the individual in predisposed, energetic ways. Understanding how the Four Worlds function and how consciousness operates within them has been a very significant part of my research.
>
> Over the past fifty years as a clinical psychologist, I delved into varied areas of therapeutic intervention to learn how

to help my clients better. With an understanding of the Four Worlds, it is now apparent that clinical tools are world-specific. Thus, it is imperative that any psychological or esoteric system be cognizant of the specific Worlds and the skills needed to access and shift their energy. As Noble Energy Maps® become more available to the public, it is my hope that the language of the Four Worlds and the knowledge that Ra Uru Hu shared and brought into the world will be upgraded in its scientific documentation and will stand as a foundational element in the validation of the Four Words as a psychological tool of transformation.

I am deeply grateful to Ra for trusting Marvin and me to carry his work forward in a way that preserves its value and integrity. My commitment is to continue this work and expand it so everyone recognizes their divinity and how we are bathed in the cosmic energy of Love daily. As Ra always said: Love Yourself.

About the Author

Dr. Eleanor® has devoted over five decades to exploring the multidimensional nature of human consciousness through her work as a clinical psychologist, researcher, and spiritual guide. Trained at the University of Chicago in the world's first interdisciplinary Social Science program, she brings together perspectives from psychology, biology, sociology, and anthropology —reflecting the Four Worlds framework she teaches.

Her approach emerged from rigorous academic research and profound personal experience, including multiple Kundalini awakenings that transformed her understanding of consciousness. She developed the Noble Energy Maps® system, which provides a comprehensive framework for understanding the energetic patterns that shape human development and expression across all dimensions of being.

Throughout her career, Dr. Eleanor® has maintained that authentic living requires integrating all aspects of our nature rather than elevating one dimension above others. Her work consistently emphasizes direct knowing over external authority, personal experience over abstract theory, and authentic expression over conformity to conditioning.

She often reminds her students: "I've never worked a day in my life because I love what I do, and I do what I love." This integration of purpose, passion, and service exemplifies the approach to living from the soul she taught and embodied throughout her remarkable journey.

Go Beyond Human Design with Dr. Eleanor's® Noble Energy Map®

Thank you for joining Ra Uru Hu, Marvin, and me on this journey through Human Design source material that has profound implications for your health and consciousness. The insights shared in these pages represent the beginning of what is possible when you fully understand your unique, energetic makeup.

A Special Gift From Dr. Eleanor®

Discover Your Noble Energy Maps® (NEM®)

As a reader of this book, I'd like to offer you a complimentary Noble Energy Maps®, an expanded Human Design Map, personalized to reveal specific energetic patterns that are established during your early development and continue to influence you today. Noble Energy Maps® show that ninety-nine percent of the general population are Manifesting Generators here to manifest their full potential.

Your free Noble Energy Maps® includes:

- A detailed visual representation of your unique, energetic design.
- Key insights into how your early infancy development shaped your current health and decision-making patterns.

- Specific recommendations for working with (rather than against) your natural energy flow.
- Access to a private 15-minute video guide where I'll walk you through how to interpret and apply your map. Email ehp@noblesciences.com to receive a link to this video.

The Science Behind Your Design

Understanding the scientific foundation of Human Design can transform how you approach your wellbeing. Along with your Noble Energy Maps®, you'll receive my special report, The Science of Beyond Human Design, which documents aspects of Human Design that hold up scientifically.

How to Claim Your Free Gifts

1. Visit www.nobleenergymaps.com for your Free Noble Energy Maps®
2. Fill in your birth details for your personalized Noble Energy Maps®
3. Email me at ehp@noblesciences.com, and The Science of Beyond Human Design Report will be delivered to your inbox within 48 hours.

This offer is my way of helping you apply what you've learned in these pages directly to your unique situation. Your design is unique and extraordinary, and understanding it is the first step toward well-being.

May your health align with your authentic design,
In Loving Light
Dr. Eleanor®

Noble Energy Wellness®

Noble Energy Wellness® focuses on Energy Medicine and Holistic options for healing and health. Dr. Marvin and Dr. Eleanor® teach energy wellness in their weekly Manifest Your Dreams Webinar. Through the webinar, you can learn how to live authentically while manifesting your actual potential by understanding and integrating the Four Worlds into your daily life. Register to learn how you can manifest your dreams by attending these weekly webinars.
https://www.nobleenergywellness.com

Noble Energy Maps®

Noble Energy Maps® focus on Dr. Eleanor's proprietary and innovative system for mapping how cosmic energy impacted you during your childhood development and how you can use this knowledge to optimally time your decisions, identify your life purpose, and live a self-realized life. Dr. Eleanor® statistically validated her system through over 45,000 cases and uses Noble Energy Maps® to guide clients toward wholeness and empowerment.
https://www.nobleenergywellness.com/energy-map/

The Noble Logo has a special place in Dr. Eleanor's heart. Her first cat, Noble, lived to age 22 and was an inspiration and guide during important times in Dr. Eleanor's growth and studies. He worked with her and Dr. Marvin when they hosted weekend groups for over ten years. Noble always helped guide them toward whom to work with next, as well as to the area that clients needed to work on. Dr. Eleanor® uses calculations based on research done on her two homegrown twin kittens. The critical human developmental times used in Dr. Eleanor's proprietary maps, have proven accurate clinically and statistically, which map the Four Worlds in your energy field and how you can best function.

The Mandala of Synthesis® describes the elements coded into Dr. Eleanor's proprietary Noble Energy Maps®. The Mandala of Synthesis includes the Kabalistic Tree of Life, Chakras, Astrology, the Hexagrams of the I-Ching, and critical times in early Human Development. Dr. Eleanor® calculates her maps and integrates the information coded into a graphic illustrating the way you use your energy, where the flow of energy becomes clear. Dr. Eleanor's extensive education as a social scientist, researcher, and clinician has empowered her to formulate a complete system that recognizes the complexity of your consciousness and shows how you can best use it for growth and expansion of consciousness.

https://www.nobleenergywellness.com/mandala-of-synthesis

www.ingramcontent.com/pod-product-compliance
Lightning Source LLC
Chambersburg PA
CBHW070104080526
44586CB00013B/1186